1 2 3
READ!

A Step-by-Step
Tutoring Plan for Teachers,
Parents, and Friends

Judith H. Dettre
University of Nevada, Las Vegas

Fearon Teacher Aids
Carthage, Illinois

Dedication

This book is dedicated to the hundreds of young and not so young
people who helped me develop these strategies, as tutors and as
tutored; and to my husband, who hardly griped at all while this was
being written.

Edited by Beverly Cory
Text and cover designed by Susan True
Copyright © 1980 by Fearon Teacher Aids, 1204 Buchanan
Street, P.O. Box 280, Carthage, Illinois 62321. All rights
reserved. No part of this book may be reproduced by any
means, transmitted, or translated into a machine language
without written permission from the publisher.
ISBN-0-8224-5788-1
Library of Congress Catalog Card Number: 79-52661
Printed in the United States of America.
1.9 8 7

Contents

Why This Book Was Written

You may be wondering, "Who is Judith Dettre and why did she write this book? What does she know about reading, anyhow?"

I work at the University of Nevada, Las Vegas, in the Department of Special Education. I teach teachers and future teachers how to work with youngsters and adolescents who have learning problems. I also oversee the department's Learning Lab—a place where university students work with public school pupils who have learning problems.

Would you care to guess the number 1 problem that brings these youngsters to the Learning Lab? It's the same problem that the university students seem least able to handle, and the one that parents of children in the Learning Lab want the most advice about. Reading? Bet on it!

The orthodox systems for teaching reading (the regular elementary programs plus the many excellent remedial programs available) work fine for up to 95 percent of the public school population. But we don't see that 95 percent in the Learning Lab. We see the hard-core 5 percent who manage to defy the system. They've slipped through both sieves; they're floundering and getting older every day.

Pretty soon you'll be saying, "This book is terse and blunt." Yes, it certainly is. It's that way because the Learning Lab pupils are getting older and more impatient every day, and so am I.

They need help, with no frills, and *now.* My job—perhaps compulsion—is to help the helpers of those problem readers fast, before another crop of Learning Lab pupils, parents, and university students gives up—or before I do. That's why I originally wrote this book.

When I decided to get on with it, I also decided I wasn't going to spend a lot of time justifying or qualifying what I said. Simplicity became the word of the day—which is why some of my terms don't jibe with standard reading jargon. I also found that stating things rather strongly kept me awake. My efforts may make you mad or glad, but another "ho hum" book we don't need.

This book will not snow you with technical jargon and $64,000 words. I'd like to impress you with the system, not my vocabulary. This book will not stress research data. The system is based simply on what it takes to learn to read, and it grew out of years of experience in helping problem readers. It is an ongoing system— one that I am continually refining even as this book goes to press. The researchers can take over where I leave off, but meanwhile, the teaching has to begin.

Now *you* have the book, and with it my system for teaching basic reading. My message to you is the same as it has been to my helpers in the Learning Lab over the years: We are not going to wait for the specialist—we are going to help that problem reader read better now. Believe it. If you can't believe it, at least clear your mind and withhold judgment for a while. Otherwise, see if you can turn this book in and get your money back.

This book will show you how to help a problem reader of any age—right now, today, or tomorrow—depending on how much time you have to study today. You will become familiar with a very simple system for teaching reading, one that is stripped to its bare bones. You will be able to help a person with real reading difficulties without benefit of courses in how to teach reading, previous experience, or expensive materials. You *will* need to study this skinny little book carefully; round up some easy-reading books, papers, magazines, or any pages of print handy; and get some unlined index cards, pencils, marking pens, and a few other similar items. And you'll need to believe that you can do the job. I *know* you can.

JUDITH H. DETTRE

All You Need to Know to Start

What Happens When You Read?

At some time in the past, you and I learned to read—but do you remember how you did it? Probably not. You'll do your job better now, though, if you take a few minutes to bring some of those processes back to mind. A situation that faces you with some difficult reading will help.

Suppose your doctor has just informed you that your 12-year-old has Osgood-Schlatter's disease. The doctor tried to explain it, but you didn't really get many of your questions answered, and you still feel ignorant about what's causing your youngster's sore knees and limp. You consult a medical book, and find the following:

> Osgood-Schlatter's disease is a form of osteochondrosis affecting the tibial tubercle. The resulting fragmentation of the epiphysial center involves an area of poorly calcified and rapidly growing bone surrounded by a densely calcified ring. If weight bearing is continued there may be fragmentation of the center, ending in malformation.

As you were reading, you tried to recognize each written word by matching it with a familiar spoken word. This process of silently pronouncing words is called *decoding*. To decode the passage on Osgood-Schlatter's disease, you rapidly went through several steps.

Forty of the words in the 49-word sample you just read were familiar to you—*disease, area, form, by,* and so on—and your first step was to register them in your mind. You knew them on sight, so they are part of what is called your *sight vocabulary.* A few other words—*calcified, fragmentation,* and *malformation*—may have needed a second glance, since you probably don't see them every day.

Then there were the goodies which, unless you're a nurse or a med school dropout, required *word attack: osteochondrosis, tibial, tubercle,* and *epiphysial.* When you first came to each of these in the selection, you probably kept on reading, hoping that the rest of the sentence would help you figure them out. This is called *decoding from context clues.* The context consists of the words, sentences, and thoughts around the unknown word. When you are familiar with an idea and the way it's being said, one unknown word can often be decoded—or at least the meaning determined—using the context around it.

But in this example, the context didn't help much. There were frequent unknown words, the reading material was quite different from your speech, and all the unknowns appeared in the first sentence. So you no doubt shifted into second gear with your next decoding approach. You broke *osteochondrosis* (for example) down into smaller units: *osteo-chon-dro-sis.* This technique—decoding the separate parts of a word and then pulling them back together—is called structural analysis. Having done that, you could now at least *say* the word. You probably went back and read the sentence again, hoping context would now supply the meaning. If it didn't, you shifted into third gear and tried to supply meanings for each separate part of the word. Let's say you decided that the prefix *osteo* had something to do with bones, as it does in *osteopath.* And you knew that the suffix *sis* means "malfunction" or "disease," as in paraly*sis.* But what about *chondro?* You remember the word *hypochondriac,* but there *chondro* also seems to mean just "disease." At this point you may have settled for "bone disease or malfunction" and gone on. Or you might have given up, particularly since you saw *tubercle* and *epiphysial* coming up.

In rapid order, here are some important points about this reading experience:

- You first tried to decode the selection by supplying a known spoken word from your inner word bank for each printed word you saw. In other words, you tried to use your sight vocabulary.
- You then applied word-attack skills. You used (or tried to use) context clues and structural analysis to help you decode the words you didn't know on sight.
- When you could pronounce all the words, you had finished decoding.
- But you, the experienced reader, were thinking about the total meaning of the passage while you were decoding. The beginner can't handle this. Almost all of the beginner's concentration is needed just for decoding words. There's very little left to ponder the meaning at the same time. Only after material is decoded can the beginner apply attention to the meaning of the passage—to *reading comprehension.*
- If it took you longer than 5 seconds each to figure out *osteochondrosis, tibial, tubercle,* and *epiphysial,* the selection was on *frustration level* for you. The experienced reader can handle this for short periods—the beginner can't. You'll learn lots more about frustration level later, but for now, focus on how hard it was for you to read about Osgood-Schlatter's disease. You may have even decided to skip the whole thing, and this is typical. It's amazing how the refrigerator calls when you're trying to read at frustration level. I'm emphasizing this because the person you'll be tutoring is constantly faced with frustratingly difficult material—just as you were in the Osgood-Schlatter sample.

What Does It Take to Read?

From reading about Osgood-Schlatter's disease, we can come up with some pretty straightforward steps:

- You must be able to decode a printed page, which means you know most of the words on sight—right away, no fooling around—*and* you must be able to figure out the few words on the page that you don't know.

- You must be able to decode a printed page fast enough and easily enough to concentrate on what's being said.

- You must be able to understand (comprehend) and, if appropriate, react to what's being said.

These skills are presented in their necessary order. If you can't decode, there's the ball game right there. If you can't decode rapidly and easily, comprehension is usually not achieved. (What *does* cause Osgood-Schlatter's disease?)

Learning to read involves learning to recognize certain printed words on sight, learning how to figure out new words, picking up ease and speed in decoding, and understanding and responding to what is read. Most educators will agree there's no problem with *what's* important. The infernal sticky wicket comes with *how* and *when* to do these things. How an individual will best learn to decode words is a particularly hot item. Reading specialists conduct studies and just plain argue year after year. Alas, none of them can crawl inside a beginning reader's head and know for sure which method *that* reader is using, because it may or may not be the method that is being presented. Learners are notorious for figuring out their own ways to learn.

That's why I'm giving you a relatively method-free system, one that gives the learner the most possible latitude in finding a way to get the job done. This approach is particularly important for your learner because he or she hasn't learned with the standard methods, right? So I'll place a great deal of emphasis on *what's important,* make some specific suggestions about *when* it's important to do those things, but treat *how* like a controlled smorgasbord. I might say, for example, "Here are 75 important words the reader should learn right away. Try to have your reader learn 4 words per session; learning the 75 words should take him or her 20 to 30 sessions. If the pupil can't learn the words without help, try this. . . . If that doesn't work, try this. . . ." And so on.

Which brings us to my system, and what it's all about.

Decoding Level Survey—Sample B

Jack and Lisa had a cousin who was
visiting them. Cousin Andy had a brand-
new car and he wanted to show off.

Andy backed the car out of the driveway
and headed for the lake. He liked to drive
fast, so pretty soon they were going
60 . . . 65 . . . 70.

Lisa was upset. She said, "You better slow
down and watch for police cars!"

"No problem," Andy laughed. "I can pick
them up on my CB."

The car went flying over a hill, and
there sat a police car waiting for them.

"He must have a CB, too." said Jack.

The Stage I reader's program consists of learning 75 to 100 sight words, including at least 50 of what I call *basic utility words*. In addition, this reader gains experience in guided connected reading. Listening comprehension and prereading word-attack skills are added as time permits. After no more than 30 sessions, the Stage I reader graduates to Stage II or is placed there.

The Stage II Reader

- knows more than 75 words on sight
- knows how to figure out a few unfamiliar words, but not consistently
- can decode a first reader but not an easy third-grade book
- doesn't like to read

The Stage II reader continues to learn sight words, but there is a greater emphasis on connected reading, word-attack skills, and reading comprehension. Stage II work is probably more like traditional remedial reading instruction than any other stage, but there are some differences. Reading *to* and *with* the problem reader is stressed as much as reading alone, and word-attack skills are included only as needed.

The Stage III Reader

- can decode at least an easy third-grade book
- can figure out most unfamiliar words
- can't decode rapidly or smoothly, and often can't understand or use what is read
- *really* doesn't like to read

Stage III is the place for increasing speed, ease, and, most of all, confidence. The program here is largely devoted to guided reading practice and silent reading with a purpose. Reading comprehension and study skills get a lot of emphasis.

Reading Sessions at the Different Stages

The suggested time allotment chart shows how a half-hour reading session might go, according to which stage your reader is in. You can see what skills you will be working on, and a suggested time allotment is given for each skill.

Suggested Time Allotments For
Half-Hour Reading Session

	15 minutes Learning Words	5 minutes Connected Reading	5 minutes Word Attack Skills	5 minutes Listening Comprehension
Stage I				

	5 minutes Learning Words	10 minutes Connected Reading	5 minutes Comprehension	10 minutes Word Attack Skills
Stage II				

	15 minutes Connected Reading	15 minutes Comprehension/Study Skills
Stage III		

Don't try to memorize all this. The chart is presented here as an overview of what you'll be doing, and to show the balance of types of work at different stages. You can bet you haven't seen the last of it!

Picking Out Books and Materials

Anything with printed words on it, including books, magazines, the yellow pages, directions on shampoo bottles, traffic signs, and the Sears catalog, can be useful in teaching a number of aspects of reading. But for decoding practice, books are your best bet.

There's nothing sacred about the reading books used in schools and, unless you're careful, using them can hinder your progress as much as help. For example, you may think you have to work your way through every book in a series of school reading books, or *basal readers,* page by page. That's just what you don't have to do. *You can skip from book to book and from series to series.* This gives you a lot more choice in finding books that interest your reader. But a word of caution is in order here. If you have to choose between material that is on your reader's decoding level and material that your reader is wildly interested in, pick the decoding-level stuff. Wild interest will pale noticeably at frustration level. Of course, the best of all worlds is decodable material that turns the reader on. You may do as well finding these books in your local library as you do at your local school. Dr. Seuss, easy joke books, and *The Guinness Book of World Records* (for Danny) should not be considered second-class materials.

To round out this section on books, let me just say that I'm all for them. Language experience fanatics (they're the ones who favor having the reader work on his or her own spoken material, suitably written out by a tutor or teacher) have a different viewpoint. I knew a professor who kept insisting that all he needed to teach reading was the sand in the desert and a stick to write with. I doubt it. You can kid a beginner along for a while with handwritten, dictated stories and the like, but sooner or later the reader is going to want something with a little more prestige value. Who's kidding whom? The whole idea behind reading is decoding someone else's written language, not your own.

Using the 100-Word Method

Whatever your source of reading material, you'll need to try it on your reader for size (difficulty). You're always in search of material at the reader's decoding level, and basically all you need to remember is the magic formula: 3 to 7 words missed per 100 = decoding level. Whenever the miss rate goes below 3 words per 100, you know the material is easy for your reader; whenever it goes above 7 per 100, you're working with material that's on frustration level, and you need to find something easier. (At first you'll need to count out 100-word samples [from the middle of a book you're considering, for example] and mark up a photocopy of the sample with the words your reader misses, as you did with your first placement tests.) Pretty soon, however, you will be able to accurately determine decoding level in your head. You will internalize what 3 to 7 misses in 100 words—or about 1 miss in 20—sounds and feels like. Presto, you have a built-in decoding-level detector. You will also recognize when your reader is missing 8 or more words per 100—that's your built-in frustration-level detector.

These internalized level detectors will be your most valuable possessions. Tests and the levels written on books (if you're using school materials) can let you down, but your built-in decoding-level and frustration-level detectors won't. When your sensors tell you a book is on your reader's frustration level, you'll look for easier material. If your decoding-level detector tells you everything is A-OK, you'll keep the book you have.

Watching Your Reader's Responses

As your reader tackles a selection out loud, you'll get one of three kinds of reactions, indicating that the material is easy, average, or hard. Observing these reactions will back up your use of the 100-word-sample method.

- *Easy.* The reader misses no more than 2 of the 100 words. The reading is smooth. Both you and the reader are relaxed. The reader is decoding well without your help—independently. If you want a new term, you can say the material is on the reader's *independent decoding level.*

- *Average.* The reader misses 3 to 7 words per 100. The reading is slower with noticeable pauses. The reader isn't relaxed, but isn't squirming either. Both of you are concentrating fairly hard. This material is about right for the reader's abilities; it's on *decoding level.*

- *Hard.* The reader misses 8 or more words out of 100. The reading is slow and halting with many long pauses, or jerky with lots of repeats. The reader is squirming, rubbing an eye, trying to strike up a conversation, or all three. Both of you are looking forward to the end of the selection. The material is at the reader's *frustration level.* (Remember Osgood-Schlatter?)

Finding Easier Material

Here are some handy guidelines to give you a general idea of what makes a book easier or harder.

- *Vocabulary.* The number of different words found in a book is an important clue. A beginner book will have about 10 to 20 different words in it, repeated again and again. It doesn't matter what the 10 words are. Learning to recognize these words will give your beginner a 10-word sight vocabulary to use in connected reading. (We all have to start someplace.) In a basal reading series, this beginner book is called a first preprimer.

  A primer-level book will have 60 to 80 different words. The name of the game at this level is repetition. Listening to a book on primer level is guaranteed to drive you bananas.

  As more and more different words appear, with fewer repetitions of each word, the book gets harder. Basal readers and some other books will have a vocabulary list in the back, showing you which different words are introduced and on what page. In this way you can get a feel for how heavy the vocabulary load is. You can even try this word list on the reader first, as another check on the book's difficulty level.

- *Number of words per sentence.* This is pretty obvious. Note that the number of words *on a line* is more pertinent for the beginner than the number of words in a sentence. Most beginners need more than a little dot for a breather. A true beginner book will have 3 to 5 words per line. A third-grade book will have 6 to 10.

- *Print, spacing, and pictures.* Beginner books usually have large type and quite a bit of space between words and lines. Gradually this all changes, until at third-grade level the page looks pretty much like large-size adult material (you know, the kind advertised on the front of some paperbacks as "easy to read with large type").

And now a disenchanting thought. Pictures are not always helpful. In fact, too many can be downright distracting. Some youngsters are so dependent upon pictures that they will never learn to decode adequately until given their printed material straight. You might keep a pair of scissors handy for alteration of old books.

An excellent book to help you become familiar with different book levels is *Graded Selections for Informal Reading Diagnosis, Grades 1 through 3,* by Nila Banton Smith (New York: New York University Press, 1969). This book has short selections on all levels, from the first preprimer through hard third-grade level. It's a great tool for finding your reader's exact decoding level. Even better, it shows you just what a book on a given level will look like—vocabulary, number of words per sentence and line, print size, and so on. There's even a second volume that has selections of fourth-grade level through sixth-grade level material.

Basic Utility Words

People who study reading have discovered something interesting: No matter what reading material you use, some words will keep cropping up again and again. These words are called basic sight words, instant words, or the 100 most common words in the English language, depending on who did the study and made up the name. I've gone over several of these lists and made up my own (see page 20). The 120 basic utility words on my list are guaranteed to be important—each one appeared on at least three of the four major lists I used. *At least half of all the words in a book of any level are right there.* Without knowing them, the reader doesn't stand a snowball's chance of decoding even the simplest written material.

If the reader *knows* most of those 120 words, however, it's a different story. He or she will be able to switch from book to book, confident about recognizing a lot of words. Don't be concerned about proper names. If you're using school readers, *Randall* and *Justina* in one series will become *Mike* and *Pam* in another. And mispronouncing them won't affect decoding or meaning much. Remember Osgood-Schlatter—or was it Osmond-Schlatter? Not many youngsters have trouble with proper names anyhow. It's when they can't get words like *then* and *how* that there's trouble. And any two books will have those words and a whole lot more in common.

120 Basic Utility Words

*a	*did	*in	*one	there	work
about	do	into	or	*they	would
*after	down	*is	order	think	yes
all	find	*it	our	*this	*you
*am	*for	jump	*out	three	your
an	from	just	over	*to	
*and	funny	know	play	too	
any	*get	laugh	please	*two	
*are	*go	*like	ran	*up	
as	*good	little	red	us	
*at	got	look	rid	very	
away	*had	made	run	want	
be	happy	*make	said	*was	
been	has	*may	saw	*we	
before	*have	*me	say	well	
big	*he	much	*see	went	
blue	her	*my	*she	were	
but	here	new	so	when	
by	him	*no	*some	where	
came	his	*not	that	which	
*can	how	*now	*the	who	
come	*I	of	them	*will	
could	if	*on	then	with	

How to Write

There's a type of hand printing you should know about no matter what stage reader you are working with. It's called *manuscript writing,* and you'll use it to make word cards for your reader.

Manuscript writing is popular for beginning readers because— with three exceptions—the little letters look just like print in a

---

*The 43 asterisked words appear on all four lists. They are particularly important at all stages.

Manuscript Alphabet*

a b c d e f g h

i j k l m n o p

q r s t u v w x

y z

A B C D E F G H

I J K L M N O P

Q R S T U V W X

Y Z

---

*Reprinted by permission from *TUTOR: Techniques Used in the Teaching of Reading* by Ruth J. Colvin and Jane H. Root, copyright © 1972 by Follett Publishing Company.

book. (The exceptions are a, g, and t.) It's done mainly with circles and sticks, and it isn't all that difficult. The manuscript alphabet with how-to-do-it illustrations appears on page 21. If your reader is in Stage I or II, you'll need a set of the 120 basic utility words written on blank index cards. Why not practice your manuscript writing now and get the cards done at the same time?

Going On From Here

Your crash course in reading is finished—that is, *I* am done with it. This chapter will always be right here, waiting for your return. I'll send you back to it from time to time

Each of the next three chapters is devoted to one of the three stages in learning to read. You'll find all the nitty-gritty you need, and possibly more than you want. Read through all three chapters before settling down to work with your particular reader. And don't worry if you're not as confident as you would like to be. Working with Joe or Alice will soon put it all together for you.

Helping Joe,
A Stage I Reader

Joe's most typical characteristic is that he can't read 75 different words. On top of that, Joe can't seem to figure out (decode) new words, no matter what, and he may forget the ones he seemed to know yesterday.

If you're a teacher familiar with the process and jargon of learning to read, you would say Joe is a nonreader, or reading at preprimer or primer level. If you're his parent, you may suddenly be aware of a teacher's concerns for "maybe keeping Joe back," or of Joe's inability to read the harder Dr. Seuss books. If you're Joe's friend, you may have noticed that he can't read the directions for heating his TV dinner.

If he's older than about 10 and has been in school recently, Joe has probably done the rounds of tutors and clinics and may have picked up some grim labels like *dyslexic, remedial reader,* or *confused laterality case.* Don't let such terms frighten you. More often than not, labels become an excuse for doing nothing to help the problem reader. In any case, here are some facts you should know about terms that may have been applied to your problem reader:

- *Dyslexia* simply means a severe reading problem. Don't think of it as a permanent physical handicap. Short of an autopsy, you can't positively lay the blame for dyslexia on faulty wiring in the brain.

- You can't tell much of anything about Joe's reading until he can read something, and the older Joe is, the less likely it is that he's been given materials to read that are *really* on his level. Junior high or senior high school teachers define easy-reading materials as fourth-grade level books. If Joe is able to read only first-grade level materials, of course he's in trouble. All his school reading is on frustration level.

- If Joe sees the word *was* and calls it *saw*, there is no reason to hit the panic button. Many young beginners, particularly boys, will reverse letters and words as a matter of course during Stage I. This can be attributed to faulty attention just as easily as to anything more sinister. If left alone, most of these youngsters will stop reversing by the time they are reading on second-grade level. On the other hand, if their behavior becomes a big attention getter these children are likely to keep it up indefinitely.

- You may have been told that Joe has a reading comprehension problem. (A common term used to describe this condition is *word caller,* which implies that Joe is saying words without knowing what they mean.) It's true that Joe can't understand the meaning behind printed words—but then he can't decode them yet either. Until he can recognize a number of words on sight, he *can't* have a reading comprehension problem. Joe may be many things but at Stage I, he is *not* a word caller. He's trying to *become* one so he can graduate to having comprehension problems!

What Joe's Job Is

Clearly and simply, Joe's job is to learn to recognize 75 words on sight—in any order, in any place—within 5 seconds each, consistently.

To do his job, Joe must figure out some system for associating print on a page with sounds. Most commonly, Joe makes the association between whole printed words and whole *spoken* words. He often begins by recognizing a proper name or two—perhaps *Joe* because he sees it so often, or something with a very unusual pattern, perhaps *Sam-I-am* in an easy Dr. Seuss book. Hopefully each time he sees the same word he will make the same association and give the same response; but this depends on repetition and Joe's ability to remember.

Most people do initially learn at least a few words by this "whole-word" method. Some educators ignore this and teach "phonics first," aimed at getting a reader to concentrate on just the component sounds within words. Those readers still keep bootlegging whole words at every opportunity, though; it's hard to avoid cereal boxes and stop signs.

Naturally there are limits to the whole-word, straight memory routine. Just so many words can be stored in Joe's head. But when these limits are reached, he will be ready for Stage II where he will learn other methods of decoding words, including some phonics. Meanwhile, as I stated earlier, his job at Stage I is clearly and simply to learn to recognize at least 75 and preferably 100 words on sight—in any order, in any place—with 5 seconds each, consistently.

What Your Job Is

You are to help Joe learn at least 75 words—in any order, in any place—within 5 seconds each, consistently.

Besides directly helping him learn 75 words, you also will be working with Joe on a few other things, time permitting. But make no mistake about priorities here. Learning words comes first at Stage I.

What Your Reading Sessions Will Be Like

If Joe is anything but borderline Stage II, you can expect to have 20 to 30 sessions at Stage I. After that, Joe will go on to Stage II. If you aim for 4 new words per session, Joe will have plenty of time to pick up 75 to 100 words. Since learning words is your major goal for Stage I, it will receive the most attention. Your initial sessions will most likely be spent entirely on learning words—developing Joe's sight vocabulary.

As he goes along, Joe will most likely be able to learn his 4 words per session in less and less time. Both of you will then increasingly welcome different activities to round out the session. After a few sessions you will be adding one, two, or all of the following: connected reading, word-attack skills, listening comprehension. At the halfway point in Stage I—session 10 to 15—your half-hour reading session might be like this:

15 minutes	5 minutes	5 minutes	5 minutes
Learning Words	Connected Reading	Word-Attack Skills	Listening Comprehension

The half-hour time block is arbitrarily presented as typical for most tutoring sessions. Tutor time and pupil attention are big factors here. If the traffic will bear a longer session, the basic time allotments can be expanded proportionately—that is, at session 10, a 1-hour lesson might consist of 30 minutes of learning words and 10 minutes each of connected reading, word-attack skills, and listening comprehension. But these suggestions are only guidelines. Don't set a stopwatch or feel guilty if you miss something. Take your cues from Joe if you think an activity should be extended or shortened. Is he still benefiting from learning words practice after 15 minutes? If so, continue. If he's pretty twitchy, go on to connected reading.

If you're working with a group, a little juggling will be needed so that enough individual instruction is provided. Your readers can do some of the learning words session in pairs, and learning words can be combined, in part, with word-attack skills to give more independent work time. If your readers are on widely different levels, connected reading should be done on a one-to-one basis. Listening comprehension, on the other hand, may be a whole-group activity.

Getting Ready

Now is the time to make yourself a set of word cards if you didn't follow the suggestion to make them earlier on. Use the 120 basic utility words (listed on page 20) to practice your manuscript writing. Write each word on a blank index card. You won't be wasting your time since these words will appear often in the materials you'll be working with. Make cards even for words Joe already knows—you will need them for activities other than sight word practice.

The next thing to think about is a progress chart. If you don't know where you're going, it's awfully hard to get there. This goes double for Joe, who has been busy going nowhere for months or possibly years. It's time to chart progress in such a way that you'll both be able to watch Joe's reading ability increase.

Make a chart like the one on page 29. If time is no problem and you have the urge to create, you might want to try something more exotic. Assuming that time is a problem, here's how to use the chart I have shown:

- Each time Joe masters a word, write the word in one of the blocks on the chart.
- Right above the word in the block, write the date of mastery.
- Fill up the blocks, left to right, across the page.
- When you reach the end of a line of blocks, move down to the next line.
- It's a good idea to have Joe read the old words from the chart before writing any newly mastered ones.
- Be sure a word is really mastered before entering it.

Wórking with Joe

To work effectively with Joe, you will need two things:

- a notebook
- a *very* easy reading book (preprimer or other book with about 25 different words repeated a lot)

Schedule

The early sessions will go something like this:

Warm-up (5 minutes).   Talk with Joe about what he likes and doesn't like, including reading.

Connected reading (5 minutes).   Have Joe read from the very easy book. In your notebook, keep a list of the words he doesn't know. If Joe can't read 19 out of 20 words in the book you selected, you've missed his decoding level. Find an easier book. (You have determined, however, that he is definitely a Stage I reader.)

Utility word card test (4 minutes).   Have Joe try to say the utility word cards. Put one down in front of him and wait 5 seconds. If he doesn't come up with the word by himself, go on to the next one. Put the cards he recognizes in one pile and the ones he doesn't in another. Stop when he has missed 10 words. (If you are a teacher, you may prefer to use the Dolch Basic Sight Word Test or the Popper Words.*

Selecting words to learn (2 minutes).   Print 1 or 2 words from your notebook on index cards. These are the words Joe missed in the easy-reading book. Pick eight or nine of the utility word cards he didn't know to make a total of 10 unknown words.

---

*Dolch Basic Sight Word Cards (Champaign, Ill.: Garrard Press, 1949).

The 100-Word Chart

Getting signals straight (1 minute). Explain to Joe that he is going to learn 3 new words (or 2 or 5, depending on his age and experience) *right now.* You can have him pick the ones he wants to learn immediately, but level with him that he's going to learn them all eventually, and then some. Explain to Joe that he'll have to recognize these words "chop-chop"—no sounding out and all that jazz. He'll just have to memorize them.

Learning words (10 minutes). Put the first word card down in front of him and say the word: "This is *look.*" Let him study it a few minutes. Then ask him, "What is it?" If Joe has trouble, ask him, "How can you remember that this is *look*?" *Caution:* Make him tell *you*—don't feed him his lines. Joe may be concentrating on the number of letters in a word, the pattern the different letters make, the first letter in the word, the last letter in the word, the middle of the word, the fingerprint on the corner of the card, or the position of the word on the card—whatever it takes. He will notice more and different cues the longer he works with the word. Encourage anything he says with a "Good."

After doing this with the four cards (or two or five), mix them up and present each again. If Joe reads a word immediately (within 5 seconds), put a tally mark on the back of that card. Keep mixing the cards up until you have made at least five presentations of each card. (You can often keep his interest up with a comment like, "Darn, I thought I could fool you that time.") Don't rush it. Allow time for more studying if he's really having trouble. Ask again, "How are you going to remember that this is *look*?" Retest when he seems more confident.

Caution: Do nothing to distract Joe from his own way of concentrating on the decoding task. Tell Joe the word *only* after he's tried to get it for 5 seconds. During those 5 seconds do not say; "How does it look?", "Sound it out," "You remember . . . ," "It means the same as. . . ." *Don't say anything during the 5 seconds.* When he gets the word on time, get excited about it!

Warm-down (3 minutes). Give Joe a pep talk on how well he did. When he has made at least three correct responses for each word, stop and praise him: "See, I knew you could learn these 3 words today.'' Bring out the 100-Word Chart and really make a big deal out of it. You might pencil in the words he learned in the first blocks. Be sure to explain that he must know them the following day even quicker in order to have them written in ink.

This is an excellent time to ask Joe if he would like to practice the words on his own. If Joe is doing this work away from home, it's a great idea to make a separate set of cards for him to take with him. Don't give him a whole batch at once, though—only as many as you might expect him to know by the next session.

After each session. Copy the words from your notebook onto index cards. You can use these words with a few more of the utility word cards each time. This way you are sure to have on your cards most of the words Joe needs for his connected reading.

Watching Joe's Progress

Ideally Joe will be learning at least 3 utility words and 1 word from his connected reading each session. But don't worry if the proportions aren't precise. An equal number of utility words and the other words will still get Joe into Stage II.

Often Joe's learning rate will increase dramatically as he goes along. If he is able to handle 6, 8, or even 10 words per session—terrific! On the other hand, don't let him get by with slipshod recognition. If he really knows a word, he will be able to recognize it rapidly 20 times, with other word cards thrown in between.

Most people can and do learn words readily using this system. It is the preferred method of developing sight vocabulary for two simple reasons. First, if Joe can learn this way, it is faster and simpler for both of you. Second, Joe is free to use any system that works for him in his memorization task. You won't be giving him cues that are not right for his learning style, or pushing something that is different from a system he is using somewhere else.

However, some people need a little more direction than the preferred method gives them. If Joe's batting average is less than 2 words per session after eight sessions, it's time to ask yourself, "Is it the method that isn't working or am I getting bored just sitting there?" Be ruthlessly honest here. What is best for Joe is often very tedious for you. And who ever gave you the idea that tutoring at this level is anything but repetition, repetition, and more repetition?

If you can honestly say that your faith and optimism have remained high and Joe is still in a slump, stronger measures are in order. The next section is dedicated to you.

Other Things to Try

Bigger Rewards

Before giving up on the method suggested above, try bigger and better rewards or payola. When Joe recognizes the next word card in less than 5 seconds, clap your hands or shout "Terrific!" at the top of your lungs. If that doesn't turn him on, promise him he can quit after he does his daily word quota consecutively within 5 seconds each. Or give him the card to tear up after he has recognized it 20 times running. Or put an extra star or sticker next to the word on his 100-Word Chart, or give him a penny per word or an M&M—you get the picture.

It is only natural that a person who has had more than his share of failure at a task will need something to break down resistance to trying again. Keep in mind that some of the more blatant rewards like money and candy will be unnecessary once Joe begins to succeed consistently. You can't beat success as a reward. Don't be shy about praising a good effort or a good job. Joe won't slack off, he'll try harder. Keeping track of progress (charting) is also helpful to just about everyone. Can you imagine fully enjoying golf or bowling without keeping score?

Other Methods of Learning Words

You have been following the method carefully and Joe's still getting, say, fewer than 2 words per session, *and,* when you ask him "How will you remember the word?" he can't come up with anything very useful. If this is the case, it will be necessary to have him study each word card in one of the following ways.

Caution: Try only one of these methods at a time and keep to it for three sessions. If it works, continue it. If it doesn't, try another method for three sessions and so on. Trying even two of these at the same time is likely to undo everything you've accomplished. You can bet Joe has tried a combination approach in the past with little success.

- *Spell the word.* If he can recognize the letters, spelling a word can be one of Joe's biggest and best bridges to learning it. For example, spelling *b–e* can certainly help Joe to sound out the word. Another benefit of spelling the word is that it helps Joe zero in on the number of letters in it. In this manner he may relate numbers of letters to length of word. This spell-the-word approach, however, is impossible for him to use unless he can identify all the letters of the alphabet when they are presented randomly—that is, when you give him a letter card for *h* he says *h,* when you show him *s* he says *s,* and so on. If Joe can't do this, tie in this activity with teaching him letter names as a word-attack skill, as described on page 41.

- *Trace the word.* If Joe traces the letters with a finger, he can concentrate more fully on the particular squiggles he's faced with. After tracing the letters on the card, he can retrace them in the air if necessary.

- *Trace and spell the word concurrently.* Again, if Joe can't identify alphabet letters, forget this one.

- *Trace, spell, and write the word.* Try this only if Joe's writing skills will stand it. Don't ever let him write the word incorrectly. If he starts this, take the paper away. Have him retrace the word on the card, and spell it. Then have him write it again on the paper.*

- *Reproduce the word with letter tiles.* If Joe's writing skills are largely undeveloped, you can have him make the word with individual letter tiles, sometimes called Alphachips. (A Scrabble set will do too.) You can probably find a set at your local bookstore or you can borrow a set from a kindergarten or first-grade teacher. Give Joe the tiles that spell the word but mix them up. He must arrange them in the right order to make the word he sees in print. If you try letter tiles for three

---

*Grace Fernald has written a very useful book on this approach called *Remedial Techniques in Basic School Subjects* (New York: McGraw-Hill, 1943).

sessions and nothing happens, Joe may not see well. You might consider getting him a visual examination with a qualified optometrist or opthalmologist. Forget the tiles until after the checkup.

- *Use the letter tiles and spell the word.* Again, if he doesn't know letter names skip this approach.
- *Trace the letters on his back as he spells the word.* And hope he's not ticklish!
- *Try any further combination of spelling, tracing, and saying the word.*

In summary, very few problem readers will be unable to learn 100 words in a reasonable amount of time using the preferred method—making their own cues. But if Joe does have trouble, *don't provide more help than he needs.* For some strange reason, many people will jump right into tracing the letter when all that may be needed is to spell the word out loud. The last thing Joe needs is someone making things more difficult than they already are.

And If That Doesn't Work?

You've tried every method above, one at a time, for three sessions and. . . nothing? You didn't forget bigger rewards? What to do now? Discontinue word learning for four sessions and concentrate on connected reading, word-attack skills, and comprehension skills. (See the rest of this chapter.) Pick up word learning again on the fifth session.

Connected Reading

You tried reading with Joe during the first session mainly to see if he could read the simplest book you could find. That way you knew whether or not he really belonged in Stage I. As soon as Joe knows just 10 words, it's time to work on connected reading at each session.

The most important feature of connected reading in Stage I is practice in using the sight vocabulary Joe is building. However, almost as important is getting Joe to relax and connect his words. This will be a bigger part of reading at Stage II.

Reading from Cards

Arrange the word cards Joe knows into sentences and ask him to read them. He may try arranging the words himself and reading them aloud. For example, the first selections might go something like this:

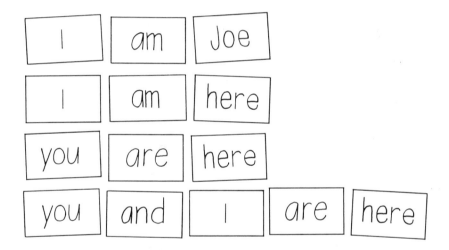

Teachers: This is a good time to use a modified language experience approach. I say modified because you need to tailor the experience to the words Joe knows as sight vocabulary.

Reading from Books

Find appropriate material.   Work with a book or books that are on Joe's decoding level. (Remember, that means he will miss only 1 word in 20.) This limits your choice at the early levels to very easy books indeed. The script in one of these books may read something like the six lines on the next page.

Look, look!

Look at Natasha.

See Natasha.

See Natasha look.

Look, Natasha.

Look at Vladimir.

The above jewel of writing has a total vocabulary of 5 different words. Joe should know the words in such a selection or should have studied each of them on cards before attempting the connected reading.

Naturally if Joe knows 50 words the choice of literature is increased. Try a book, and if Joe is missing mainly proper names, teach him those first before deciding the book is on frustration level. If you can't find easier books, try teaching him the words in the book first, or do some modeling (described on pages 38 and 59).

Have Joe read aloud.   As Joe reads aloud, follow the earlier procedure of listing in a notebook the words he misses after you tell him what they are. Don't make comments such as "Sound it out," "You know that word," and so forth. On the other hand, be sure to let him cope with the word for 5 seconds before you pronounce it for him. One of the secrets to smoother connected reading is for you to look over the selection ahead of time. Use part of your word study time to help Joe with those words you anticipate will be troublesome.

Watch the decoding level.   If Joe misses so many words that they won't fit on your notebook page, try an easier book. Joe should recognize about 20 words for every word missed. Remember that decoding level! There's one notable exception to the poor-decoding/find-an-easier book rule. In rare cases Joe's poor decoding may reflect boredom with material that is too simple. A complete lack of challenge can definitely affect concentration. When you've given easier books a fair trial and there's no improvement, you might reach for a harder book.

Relax. To help Joe relax and connect his words, *you* must be relaxed. If you can't sit beside him without quietly slipping him a word when he needs it, sit on the other side of the table without a book. Obviously praise for a job well done is essential, but don't get too rowdy about it until he has finished a passage. Your enthusiasm may disconnect an otherwise connected reading attempt.

Forget Word Attack. At this point you may want to teach Joe how to figure out the harder words. Don't. There'll be time for that later in the session, not during connected reading. Reading can never be connected if you're constantly breaking in. I strongly suspect that thousands of people all over the country who don't read smoothly can trace their performance patterns to teachers who couldn't stop interrupting them to provide some "help."

Forget silent reading. Beginners don't, won't, or can't read silently. If you have a group of Stage I readers, about all you can hope for is to have them read aloud a little more quietly than when they're reading to you. Besides, how in the wide world will you ever know if Joe is decoding accurately (that is the major purpose in Stage I, you recall) if you can't hear him pronounce the words? Silent reading in Stage I makes about as much sense as wings on a pig.

Fingers and markers are OK. It's a myth that good readers keep their hands in their laps. Joe, like any beginning decoder, needs all the help he can get to keep his place. For this purpose some teachers devise simple and even elaborate markers out of construction paper or index cards. For example, the slot marker (a narrow rectangular hole in a card) blots out everything except 3 or 4 words at a time. A plain card may be held under the line, or it may be placed above the line being decoded. This keeps Joe from meandering back to a line he has already read. You can experiment with different types and placements of markers, but don't be surprised if Joe prefers to use one of his fingers. Fingers are a lot more versatile and help him "move right in there." The body movement (of the finger in this case) helps Joe who is probably action-oriented, to keep his attention on the task. The use of markers and fingers is not so habit forming as you may have heard. As the task gets easier, Joe generally stops using them automatically, so you will probably not have to break the habit at all. Don't even *try* while he's in Stage I.

Consider modeling.   If it bothers you too much to have Joe plunge right into oral reading, read the selection to him first. This is called *modeling,* which means that you will provide a model of how that passage should be read aloud. It is one of the most painless ways for Joe to pick up decoding, especially if you read the same thing to him over and over again. After a while he will begin to recognize some of the words and chime in with you. You'll do a lot of modeling in Stages II and III. If you anticipate going mad with boredom with just straight oral reading, you might want to read up on modeling techniques now and give them a whirl (see page 59).

Remember—it's fun.   Before we leave connected reading, a word should be said for the fun a beginner can have in learning to decode. Sure Joe may have resisted reading because it was so discouraging. But don't believe that he will always—even now— have to be led through a book kicking and squalling. There is nothing quite so satisfying to a person as being able to unlock a code that has previously seemed impossible. You make it possible for Joe to succeed, and then you can enjoy watching success take over.

Word-Attack Skills

In addition to working on word learning and connected reading, you will spend some time helping Joe master certain word-attack skills. These are largely readiness activities; that is, they will help Joe get ready for the phonics and other word-attack skills he will encounter in Stage II.

By the end of Stage I, Joe should be able to:

- say all the letter names when letters are presented randomly in isolation (I didn't say letter *sounds,* I said *names!*)
- place some kind of dividing symbol between or around every word on a page of print
- find all the *d*'s, *r*'s, and so on in a page of print
- alphabetize single letters and his word cards, including several words that begin with the same letter
- find selected words on page of print
- find selected words in a simple picture dictionary
- identify isolated letter sounds when he hears them
- identify words that start with the same or different sounds when presented orally
- identify rhyming words when presented orally
- blend consonant-vowel-consonant sounds into words (such as *cat, man, sun, bed*) when presented orally

Why This Word-Attack System Is Different

Phonics. If you're over 18 and you haven't heard anything about phonics in reading, you must have been living somewhere like Outer Siberia. Now matching sounds with letters and groups of letters in words certainly is essential to figuring out unfamiliar words, no doubt about it. But a lot of reading programs have gone overboard in the last 20 years, to the point where some want to teach phonics as a separate language all its own; the term for this is *extrinsic phonics.* Some people also think that if they don't have a stack of phonics workbooks and reams of worksheets, all arranged in the right order, they can't possibly do anything to help a person learn to read.

Wrong! In many ways reading is like tennis—given a little instruction, the more you practice the better you will get. You have to get a little help with detailed skills, but you also have to get those skills into action. Now suppose the tennis pro kept you working on "proper foot position" and "proper backhand position" until you could recite the rules and position yourself automatically on command, but you were only allowed to hit a ball for five minutes a day. In short order you could talk a good game but your enthusiasm for playing would decrease. And you probably wouldn't play very well, either. The reason is obvious; to develop a skill, one must practice the skill directly and on a level appropriate to one's development.

Back to phonics and my word-attack system. My system is designed to help a person read as easily and quickly as possible. If the skill of reading can be attained without too many interruptions for phonics commercials ("Now sound it out, dear," when it's going to take a full minute), the reader may actually have time to *read*.

Keep in mind that word attack should be a means to an end and that knowledge of phonics isn't an end in itself. Of those teenagers who've had an exclusive dose of phonics, how many do you know who enjoy reading, who will actually buy a book they don't have to and sit down and read it? I rest my case.

Most beginners learn the skill of reading from a balanced combination of word-attack instruction and practice in connected reading. There are a few rugged individualists, however, who have to make up their own system of word-attack skills by practicing the total act. Trying to teach them isolated word skills is like attempting to paint a greased ceiling. For the sake of Joe—who just may be more of a rugged individualist than you guessed—don't sacrifice connected reading for word-attack skills. Balance them until you know how Joe learns best.

There is nothing magical or rigid about the order of learning word-attack skills. Specialized materials—phonics sheets and workbooks—are just as likely to be in the wrong order for Joe as in the right order. After all, he's had a good many months or years to get out of sequence. If you know the skills Joe should master in Stage I, you can find out what he does and doesn't need and go from there. This saves time and money. For example, here's a list of all the materials you will need for word-attack work at Stage I:

- word cards
- letter cards or tiles
- an individual alphabet strip or sheet (one for each person you'll be working with)

- lots of pages of print of all kinds to be ripped up, marked up, and so forth (I suggest you visit the next big "giveaway" at your local school district office)
- a marking pen or pencil
- paper
- a simple picture dictionary (one for each person)
- file box with alphabetical index for 3-by-5-inch cards (although not absolutely essential, it is useful for alphabetizing activities—try to have one for each person)
- lists of words for oral-auditory practice (see material beginning on page 47)
- books or reading materials at the proper decoding level

Basic Exercises in Word Attack

All of the following exercises should be tried with Joe if he's the only one you're tutoring. If you're working with a group, first present the task and make sure everyone understands it, then have each person do it independently. Be sure to check each person's progress from time to time, and check everyone's work after the time is up. *Teachers:* You will be glad to know that many of these activities keep a child busy longer than workbook exercises usually do!

The activities are designed to help beginning readers focus and concentrate on different aspects of letters and words so that they will be prepared for later associations. It's all very well to know the name and even the sound of the letter *b,* but if the student keeps getting the *b*'s and *d*'s mixed up, where will he or she be?

Recognition and Tracking

You'll need a few simple items for work in this area:

- pages of print from newspapers, magazines, or old books
- a marking pen or pencil
- word cards
- letter cards or tiles

To begin, show Joe one letter card or tile—choose a letter he doesn't know—and say the letter name: "This is *t.*" Then say,

"Now Joe, what is this?" After you're sure he knows the letter, pull out a page of print, put the letter card or tile at the top, hand Joe a marking pen, and have him circle every *t* on the page. Here's the clincher: Tell Joe to whisper "t" every time he circles one. (One of the biggest things you can do for youngsters is teach them to whisper.) If you want to throw in a little math, have Joe count the number of *t*'s he finds on that page.

If you really want to get all possible benefit from this exercise, introduce *tracking* as well as letter recognition. Tracking means going from left to right across the page. When Joe is able to keep his eyes moving automatically in one basic direction, his connected reading will be smoother. Chances are excellent, too, that he will not lose his place so often. Put an *X* on a page of print where you want Joe to start, draw an arrow pointing to the right above the first line, then show him how to come back to the left side every time he finishes a line. If Joe has trouble getting back to the left side after finishing a line, try an arrow on every line or several arrows on each line.

Recognition and Tracking
of the Letter

t

X ⟶

Show Joe one letter card and say the letter name. Have him put a circle around every (t) on any page of print. He is (to) whisper "(t)" every (t)ime he circles one.

Variation 1. Joe can do the same kind of exercise with words instead of letters. Put one of his word cards at the top of a page of print and have him search for it. You can't go wrong if you use the 120 basic utility words—remember how often they show up! Have Joe whisper the word each time he marks it.

Variation 1: Recognition and Tracking
of the Word

| the |

X ⟶

Joe can do (the) same thing with words instead of letters. Put one of (the) word cards at (the) top of a page of print. Put an *X* where he is to start and draw an arrow pointing right above (the) first line. Show him how to come back to (the) left after he finishes (the) first line. Ask him to whisper (the) word each time he circles it.

Variation 2.　Many beginning readers have trouble just trying to separate words on a page of print. Have Joe circle each word on a page, or put a dot or slash between each word, or underline each word, or cross out each word. Stress tracking, but don't have him whisper unless he simply says "word" for each one.

Variation 2: Recognition and Tracking
of Separate Words

X ⟶

(Have) (Joe) (circle) (each) (word) (on) (a) (page) – or·put·a·dot·between· words – or/use/slash/marks – or underline each word – or cross out each word. This/exercise/will/help/him/separate/ words/on/a/page/of/print. (Don't) (have) (him) (whisper) (the) (words).

Variation 3.   When Joe knows 50 to 100 basic utility words, give him a page of fairly adult written material. Have him underline every word he knows and whisper each one. Don't put any cards down. This exercise is usually a big morale booster since Joe probably didn't have any idea he knew so many words. It's also a good way to get him to be serious about working on the basic utility words.

Copying

Again, you'll need a few props:
- reading books or other reading materials on the proper decoding level
- a marking pen or pencil
- paper
- word cards
- separate words cut from a printed page of easy words

In this exercise you will work on word attack by having Joe practice writing letters and words. For example, on the day Joe finds all the letter *t*'s on a page of print, also have him trace and write the letter *t* several times. When he is able to write most of the alphabet easily, have him copy his beginner book—the one he's reading from. Start out with small doses and stop before he's exhausted.

Now why in the world would you do anything so boring? Because it will help Joe to look very closely at the sequences of letters he's been coming across and cement them in his brain. The only catch is that you must be on the alert for mistakes. This method will cement *them* in, too! For you skeptics, I'd like to testify that at least 10 out of 30 first graders I once taught copied their entire first preprimer. What's more, they were proud of their efforts and insisted on reading from the copy.

Variation 1.   Joe may enjoy putting his word cards in the right order to form the sentences in his reading book, rather than writing them. The only problem here is that he's going to run out of word cards pretty fast unless you make a whole batch of extras.

Variation 2. You can photocopy a page of his reading book, then cut out all the words. Have Joe paste them on a sheet of paper in the same order as the original. Sight-saving or other very large print materials are best for this.

Variation 3. Joe may also sequence letter tiles under his word cards, a process you may have already tried during the learning words session.

Alphabetizing

Here you'll need:
- letter cards or tiles
- an individual alphabet strip or sheet
- word cards
- a file box with alphabetical index
- a very simple picture dictionary

Alphabetizing is one of those study skills that keeps cropping up again and again. Here you can use it to help Joe zero in on letter shapes as well as to develop a system he's going to need later anyway. Keep in mind that identifying letter names in random order (*t* is "tee" and *d* is "dee") is not the same task as naming the letters in order. Joe will need both these skills.

Give Joe a copy of the alphabet. One way is to tape the cut-out letters in one long line across his desk or work table. Then mix up the letter tiles and have him place them in order directly under the matching letter in the alphabet. Since there are apt to be several *k*'s, a whole batch of *a*'s, and so on in the letter tiles, you might want to take out a few.

Variation 1. Give Joe the tiles for every letter of the alphabet except one. Have him find out as quickly as possible which letter is missing. You can have a race against the clock if you want to add some excitement.

Variation 2. Seat Joe on the floor and string out the letter tiles into an alphabet about 5 feet long, with lots of space between letters. Then have him alphabetize his word cards under the letters.

Or put four or so letter tiles on his desk, shuffle his word cards, and have him find all the words that start with those letters.

Variation 3.   A file box with an alphabetical index is a good way to ease into the dictionary activities Joe will be doing. Give Joe several of his word cards and see if he can stuff them in the appropriate slots. When he can do this, increase the number of cards until he can pack them all away.

Variation 4.   A final variation is to give Joe about 10 of his word cards and a very simple picture dictionary, and have him find each of the words on his cards in the dictionary. When he finds a word, have him slip the card in that page. To check, ask him to show you where he found each word. *Caution:* First be sure that all the words are in the dictionary.

Teaching Auditory Discrimination

The first step to using phonics in reading is recognizing similarities and differences in spoken words. This is called *auditory discrimination,* and Joe learns it through listening. There are a lot of conflicting opinions running around about how auditory discrimination abilities develop. Here's my position. You can help someone develop auditory discrimination abilities, but you should stay away from gimmicks because they're a lot of bother and they don't always help. The point is, if you have real problems in auditory discrimination you need your sounds straight, and you need to concentrate on them alone. The auditory exercises that follow involve relatively pure listening. *Parents:* These exercises may be done while waiting for service in restaurants or inching up to the drive-in window at the bank. They've saved my sanity many a time.

Auditory Discrimination Exercise

You will need:
- maybe the word lists that follow
- possibly a blindfold
- probably nothing

To a group or to just Joe, say, "I'm going to London and I'm going to take a bear and a banana. Do you want to go?" Joe should say that he does indeed want to go, and will take a bus or a bridge or something else that starts with the same sound.

Let's say Joe doesn't know what you're driving at with your bears and bananas. First, tell him the trick. "Listen, Joe, *bear* and *banana* start with the same sound." Run it by him again, exaggerating the initial *b* sound. If he still doesn't get it, have him watch your lips. Then have him listen to the words with his eyes closed, because that's harder and more like what he'll have to do in reading.

Variation 1.   If Joe finds bears and bananas too difficult, introduce two widely different sounds, such as *f–f–f* and *m–m–m*. Have Joe hum *m–m–m* softly to himself and ask him if *f–f–f* is the sound he's making. Then ask if it's *m–m–m*. You can say a batch of words that start with *m* while he's voicing the sound, then throw in a non-*m* word, which should cue him to raise his hand or shake his head or react in some way. You can do this with small groups, too. It's good to have a list of words ready ahead of time.

Variation 1: Auditory Discrimination

Say the words to Joe. Have him shake his head when he hears the one that doesn't start the same as the others.

1. go, gun, see, gate	6. day, dog, dance, claw
2. cat, can, cook, fun	7. make, men, sand, might
3. pat, pick, pair, dog	8. ring, rat, tell, roar
4. hill, hair, took, house	9. bat, big, box, cold
5. wink, was, won, play	10. no, nest, near, gun

Variation 2.   Many children find it easier to identify rhyming words than words that have the same beginning sound. If you think such an exercise would be helpful, try this: "I'm going to Rome and I'm taking a cat and a hat. Do you want to go?" Joe might say, "Yep, I'll take a bat . . . or a rat . . . or a gnat."

Variation 3.   You can do an easier exercise with rhyming words by presenting a list of rhyming words to which you've added one oddball. Tell Joe to react when he hears the word that doesn't rhyme. For example, say, "Scold, mold, gold, way." Joe should raise his hand or shake his head when he hears *way.*

Variation 3: Auditory Discrimination

> Say the words to Joe. Have him identify the word that doesn't rhyme with the others.
>
> 1. sill, hill, dog, kill
> 2. may, sway, day, took
> 3. hill, bill, fan, mill
> 4. squaw, draw, fold, claw
> 5. make, take, cake, pink
> 6. vent, spent, fun, cent
> 7. fell, well, smell, tall
> 8. rat, cat, hat, get
> 9. fun, bun, man, nun
> 10. chin, thin, pen, win

Variation 4.   After you've tried the above exercises a number of times and feel that Joe has the idea, you can do two more variations. The first is a blending exercise with what are called *c-v-c* words (consonant-short vowel-consonant words). You can use words like *hit, mad,* and *hum,* but draw out the sounds, for example, say *"h—ih—t,"* for *hit. Caution:* Get off the first sound of *h*

Variation 4: Auditory Discrimination

> Here Joe should blend sounds into words. You draw it out; have Joe put it together.
>
> 1. t—o is _____
> 2. s—ee is _____
> 3. n—o is _____
> 4. i—n is _____
> 5. t—u—g is _____
> 6. s—a—d is _____
> 7. bl—a—ck is _____
> 8. l—e—t is _____
> 9. c—u—p is _____
> 10. r—a—n is _____

words without an "uh." Don't say "huh"—say "h–h–h," and clip it. After you have drawn *hit* out into *h—ih—t,* have Joe try pulling it back together again into *hit.* Some people call this exercise "say-it-fast" or "say-it-together." Keep in mind that the longer the interval between sounds, the harder the task, so start out by saying the sounds with short intervals.

Variation 5.   The final variation is much like a common auditory discrimination test used by professionals, so you might think of it as a graduation exercise. Give Joe pairs of words that are either the same word twice (*mad-mad* or *pen-pen*) or differ by only one sound (*mad-bad* or *pin-pen*). Have Joe respond by saying that the sounds are the same or different. Once he can do that without watching your lips he has a fighting chance of understanding phonics in reading, which he will have to do in Stage II.

Variation 5: Auditory Discrimination

Have Joe say whether the words are the same or different.

1. moo—new	6. sack—sap
2. pin—pen	7. red—red
3. sat—sad	8. chain—chain
4. bill—bill	9. stool—school
5. trend—friend	10. bet—bit

Summing Up

This section began with a list of word-attack skills to be stressed during Stage I. You might want to review them once more before moving on to listening comprehension. The only additional point I'd like to make here is about the auditory discrimination exercises. If Joe has real trouble with them, you might want to see about a hearing checkup for him. Problems with hearing could affect Joe's performance in auditory discrimination and in listening comprehension too.

Listening Comprehension

Reading—*the whole thing*—is simply a combined process of decoding printed material, understanding what it says, and being prepared to respond to it. Reading comprehension is a combination of understanding what is decoded and being able to do something about it. For the beginner, the heavy emphasis is on understanding and thinking about what he or she has just decoded, but there is a big problem here. Beginners can't read but they can talk and think, so their reading material is usually far beneath them, both in ideas and vocabulary. After your connected reading work on the script about Natasha and Vladimir, you can see why I'm not going to waste much effort on preprimer content. If you can't get much more out of it than "What did Natasha say to Vladimir?" (answer: "Look, Look!"), don't waste your time!

Joe needs to practice understanding and thinking about material that is too hard for him to read, so one of the neatest things you can do for him is to read to him. Choose a short selection, perhaps a very short story in a book or an article in *Reader's Digest,* and follow it up with questions. The following examples of questions are based on "The Three Little Pigs"—not because that story is necessarily right for Joe, but because you're familiar with it. Once you understand the different types of questions you should ask, you can make them up for anything from recipes to TV programs.

- *Recall questions.* "What did the first little pig use to build his house?" A straight recall question will have an answer that you can read to Joe—no heavy thought should be required.

- *Translation-sequencing questions.* "Joe, can you tell me the story in your own words?" This type of question has two main purposes: (1) to enable Joe to translate the material he has heard (or, eventually, that he has read himself) into another form, the easiest of which is Joe's own spoken words (other forms that may or may not be appropriate include acting it out or drawing pictures), and (2) to help Joe organize ideas he has just heard or read so that he can hold onto them. A brief listing of events in order will do this for most people.

- *Summary questions.* "Can you make up a new name for the story 'The Three Little Pigs'?" (Possibly "A Strong House Is Best.") Joe needs to be able to condense material he has heard or read. Getting down to the bare bones of a passage or story won't be easy for him since he has spent too many years believing that every word is important. Help him by giving him limits such as "Tell me a new name in 5 words or less."

- *Vocabulary questions.* "What does *huff* mean?" Most of us have vivid memories of vocabulary drills—page after page of lists of words and a dictionary. At Stage I Joe's vocabulary development is completely dependent upon someone explaining words he hears. As you read to him, stop from time to time and explain what some of the words mean. Then ask him later to tell you what they mean.

- *Inference questions.* "Did the pigs live in the country or in the city?" An inference question requires a leap into the unknown, since the answer is not specifically given in the story. Here Joe will have to put together several knowns (there were sticks and straw around, the pigs went to a fair, and the story doesn't mention any other houses around) to guess that the answer to your question is "country." Encourage Joe to guess at answers that are not given in the material read.

- *Critical-thinking questions.* "Could a wolf blow a house down? Why not?" might get things going. Stay away from yes-or-no questions, such as "Did you like the story?" Unfortunately, this question almost always discourages true critical thinking unless Joe really feels at ease with you. (An answer of "Yeah" will usually get the tutor off his back.) You're better off with "Do you think this really happened?" or "Could this happen here?" If there is to be critical thinking, there must be a choice of answers so that Joe can use his judgment. Discussing TV commercials is a great way to practice. (Do *all* dogs gobble up Bow Wow Dog Chow? Does Squeezy Orange Drink taste as good as real orange juice?)

It will come as no great surprise that the largest percentage by far of questions asked by teachers are recall questions. These are the easiest to think of and the most concrete to assess. You will be doing Joe a big favor by asking him all kinds of questions and helping him to arrive at answers when he has difficulty.

There is no need to limit listening comprehension to stories that you read to Joe. If you can check his TV viewing habits and watch at least one of the same shows he does, you have a ready-made question-and-answer period for your next session. Tapes of old radio programs are also great sources of material for listening comprehension exercises.

All in all, there is no need for Joe's listening comprehension to stagnate at his current decoding level if you have time to do the activities above. But remember, if something has to give, don't let it be word learning!

How Joe Graduates to Stage II

When Joe can decode 75 to 100 different words (including at least 50 basic utility words) rapidly from cards or in connected reading, he is ready for Stage II. His decoding level is now at about first grade.

As he enters Stage II, Joe should also be able to do a number of other things: (1) spell out any word he sees on a page, (2) do easy alphabetizing, (3) identify words and letters on a page while tracking, (4) be able to tell if sounds are the same or different, (5) blend isolated sounds into words, and (6) correctly answer all kinds of listening questions. Don't hold him back from graduation, though, if he can't do all these things. Just figure you'll keep at them during Stage II.

Is He Really Ready?

Every so often you'll run into a problem reader who just can't seem to learn the minimum number of words. He does better on the connected reading (comparatively speaking), but the word cards give him fits. This particular Joe, if encouraged, may be able to use the words he knows to fill in the ones he doesn't. Encouragement in this case means placing Joe in Stage II, since connected reading receives greater emphasis there. Just watch the level of materials you give him to read.

As I said earlier, the average time spent at Stage I should be 20 to 30 sessions of approximately 30 minutes each. At the rate of 4 words per session, this gives Joe plenty of time to pick up 75 to 100 words. If Joe knows only 40 words by session 20, concentrate on connected reading, word-attack skills, and listening comprehension for 5 to 10 more sessions; then graduate him to Stage II. Don't drag out Stage I longer than three months. Give it your best shot and move on with confidence!

Helping Alice,
A Stage II Reader

Alice is a Stage II reader. She knows 75 or more words (sometimes up to 200), but she is helpless in the face of a new word— particularly one with two or more syllables in it.

If you're a teacher you'd say that Alice's reading level is primer, first reader, or even easy second grade if she's a good guesser. If you're a parent, you'll equate this with Alice's always selecting Dr. Seuss books (if forced to read). She'll be having trouble with her written work if she's a third grader or above. If she is an adult, she'll need help in filling out application forms or ordering dinner from a simple menu. Chances are good that somewhere someone is suggesting remedial reading or an adult literacy program for her.

Alice's main problem is still decoding—not reading comprehension. You can safely disregard statements like "She doesn't understand what she reads" from well-meaning persons who haven't guessed that her true decoding level is first grade. Of course she can't understand material on a tenth- or even fourth-grade level. No one will ever know whether or not Alice has a reading comprehension problem until she can decode better, say at hard second-grade or easy third-grade level.

Alice's spelling and writing level will be no higher than her reading level, and will probably be lower. Her written errors will most assuredly lead someone to hint at dyslexia or a severe writing problem. But, it's futile to worry about inborn writing or spelling disabilities at this stage of the game. You can't know whether Alice has a writing problem or not until she can read better.

I've saved the most common characteristic of the Stage II reader for last. Alice will not like reading. Depending upon her temperament she may complain of a headache, say she's lost her book, look around the room, change the subject, or just fling the book across the room and storm, "I hate reading!" The older she is, the more real her feelings of inferiority will be. I've never yet met an older Stage II reader who didn't, way down deep, feel dumb—regardless of how carefully parents, teachers, and friends had tried to convince her otherwise.

What Alice's Job Is

At this point Alice must really make her sight vocabulary automatic so she never has to worry about this, look, there, *and the rest, develop a system (or two or three) that will help her decode the majority of unfamiliar words, practice a lot of decoding at her own decoding level, and gain confidence.*

As Alice progresses in Stage II, reading comprehension will come into the picture. Decoding will become automatic enough so that she can concentrate more on the meaning of what she reads.

When we left our Stage I reader (or graduated him to Stage II), we knew that he had certain things going for him. If you haven't been through Stage I with Alice, you may be at a disadvantage. However, you know she has many Stage I skills or she wouldn't be reading at primer level or above. Be sure she knows or learns letter names and see how well she does in auditory discrimination exercises. If she has trouble, Alice will need to work on these in order to make progress in Stage II.

You want Alice to develop useful word-attack systems so that when she sees something like *rep* she will be able to say it, even though she has never seen it before and it has no meaning when she decodes it. By the time she gets to Stage III, she ought to be able to figure out *reptile* either by separate syllables, by context (familiar words around it), or by a combination of the two. A large portion of this chapter—the section on word-attack skills—will show you how to help Alice move in this direction. She will definitely need more than just a whole-word approach.

By far her most important task is to banish the thought that "I'm a poor reader." She must practice and practice and practice at her decoding level. *Caution:* Remember that only 1 word missed in 20 is decoding level. I'd bet my next paycheck that most of the practice Alice has received to date is at frustration level. If you're in doubt, it's better that the material be too easy than too hard. Confidence in reading is often best built at the independent level—that's where Alice misses only 1 or 2 words in 100.

What Your Job Is

You are to help Alice complete and make automatic her basic utility sight vocabulary, help her find and practice systems of decoding that will allow her to figure out most new words, and provide her with lots of successful connected reading experience.

As decoding becomes more automatic and Alice's confidence grows, you will assist her in reading comprehension. This does not mean that you will forget listening comprehension as described in Stage I, but first things first with the printed page, and that means decoding.

What Your Reading Sessions Will Be Like

Stage II will usually take anywhere from 50 to 100 sessions. At the rate of two sessions per week, you're talking about roughly six months to a year. There is nothing hard and fast about these time limits, however. Alice may be able to figure out most unfamiliar words and read a third-grade book after 20 sessions. If so, she graduates to Stage III right then. On the other hand, she may need the full 100 sessions or even more.

Word-attack skills and connected reading are your primary targets in Stage II. Suggested time allotments are given in the chart below.

5 minutes	10 minutes	5 minutes	10 minutes
Learning Words	Connected Reading	Comprehension	Word-Attack Skills

Learning Words

The learning words session is pretty much like that in Stage I, except (1) you're even more concerned with speed and ease, and (2) you make sure Alice knows every last one of the basic utility words. In Stage I she may have had about 50 of them down fairly well. Now we're after 120, zip-zip-zip! Interestingly enough, this is the easiest way I know to enable a person to handle hard second-grade-level reading material. If Alice has the 120 words down automatically, she will be reading that well.

Besides the 120 basic utility words, there will be others that crop up again and again. The Dolch list that teachers often use has 220 basic words, and if Alice knows all of these she will read on third-grade level. However, if you make cards for the words that keep giving Alice fits, dollars to doughnuts many of them will appear on the Dolch list. There's no sense borrowing trouble—Alice will still be reading on third-grade level with her own 220 sight words. The key word is *sight,* and that means *automatic.* Do not settle for anything less.

The other words you will be working on, time permitting, are those in Alice's connected reading for the day. Eventually you will want her to decode these on the spot with the skills she picks up during word-attack time. At the beginning of Stage II, however, Alice will still be applying the whole-word approach. As long as this is the case, help her learn new words in advance so she won't fall on her face during connected reading. More failure she doesn't need!

I'm not going to repeat all the jazz about learning new words. Review the suggestions in Stage I (page 32) if you're in doubt. Keep in mind that you still don't say "Sound it out," "You know that one," and so on. Sight is sight.

Connected Reading

Connected reading for Stage II stresses modeling—that's where you come in. You are the reading model. Although there are many ways to model, this section will feature two major methods and a few variations.

Modeling Method 1

The challenge.   Open a book at Alice's decoding level to an appropriate page or paragraph. Place a penny, sticker, M&M, or chart in front of Alice and say, "You are going to read this page (paragraph) perfectly—with no mistakes. When you do, you will get this (indicate payola). First I'm going to read it to you. Then you can ask me any words you don't know. Then you will read it out loud."

You don't believe me? Before you tear up this book, read a few more lines. Alice's main problem is still decoding, and she is convinced she's a klutz when it comes to reading. You must break through this cloud and get her to concentrate on something besides her previous inability. That's what the payola is for. If money turns her on, give it—particularly if you're a parent. Believe me, it's cheaper than a paid tutor! If your system cannot tolerate money or if Alice is over 14, put a mark on a progress chart. A wooden bead to be added to a necklace or leather thong might be even better. Alice needs proof of accomplishment—it makes failure easier to forget.

Speaking of proof, record Alice's oral reading on tape early in the game. Do this even though it's painful for everyone concerned. Put the tape away and bring it out in about a month or even two months if you're in no hurry. At that point make a second tape of Alice reading the same selection. Then play them both. The results will make both you and Alice feel 10 feet tall.

The performance.   To start modeling, read the chosen selection aloud, placing your finger on the title or first word and following along all the way through. It may take a little practice, but keep your finger on the exact syllable you're reading. Most beginners to this system tend to read either too fast or too slow. Make it natural and relaxed. You are the reading model.

When you've read the entire selection, tell Alice to go over it silently for words she doesn't know. (She probably won't find any the first time or two.) Then have her read it out loud.

To get the payola, Alice's reading must be perfect. It must be smooth, with no repetitions—nothing but one word after the other all the way through. Be hard-nosed. You're doing Alice no favor by giving her the payoff when her reading isn't perfect. If she goofed, say matter-of-factly, "You did well but you missed *dolphin.* Now we'll try it again." Then repeat the entire procedure, or shorten the selection if you think it's too much for her.

Also, remember the suggestions for helping Joe pay attention (page 36). What was true for Joe is true for Alice. If she keeps looking back at what she has already read, try putting a marker over the top of the line she's reading. Cover up the pictures. Let her keep her place with her finger.

The payoff.   When she does it right, get very excited, *besides* paying off. Alice will get just as much of a boot out of your compliments as she will from money or checks on a chart. She might start saying to herself, "Hey, Alice. That was pretty good. You're not so dumb after all!" Then you'll have it made.

Modeling Method 2

Method 2 is used when Method 1 makes Alice uncomfortably anxious or when you're working with a group of Alices. It goes like this:

- Read a short selection to Alice—one that is on her decoding level.
- Read the entire selection once more, keeping your place with a finger and insisting that Alice follow with her eyes.
- The third time through, either ask Alice to read aloud with you or select a few parts for her to read aloud alone.
- The fourth time through, you and Alice read alternate paragraphs.
- The fifth time, proceed just as you did in Method 1, that is, aim for perfect accuracy with no help and all words correct within 5 seconds.

If you're working with a group, they can accomplish the above either by taking turns or by working in unison. Again, use a payoff for perfection.

Some Modeling Variations

An interesting variation of the reading model is to tape-record stories on Alice's decoding level. This puts Alice in control of the number of times she repeats the reading. If you're working with a group, headsets are a necessity. Even if you're working with just one Alice, the headset may be worthwhile. Outside of an isolation booth there's no better way to shut out the world. As you are recording, be sure to sound a buzzer or bell when Alice is to turn the page so she'll know where you are if she loses the place.

One of the neatest tricks I know in providing reading models for teen-agers and adults is to write out the words to popular songs. The second neatest trick is to find some rock star who doesn't mumble. I've always liked Barbra Streisand and Carole King who I guess can't be true rock stars because on their records you can understand the lyrics. Some records even come equipped with sheets of lyrics that will make your job much easier.

Also, poetry has some definite value for modeling—particularly the old-fashioned kind that rhymes! Here the lines are of relatively consistent length, and the stanza format gives Alice a better chance of keeping her place.

Keep at it!   Do as much connected reading with Alice as you possibly can. If you're working with five people at once, it may be better to have them model in unison for 10 minutes rather than split the time in fifths. Surprisingly, Alice may be more relaxed with this McGuffey reader-type approach than with reading orally by herself. Don't worry about taking some time from other exercises. Alice will learn as much about decoding by practicing the whole skill as she would by learning its separate parts. Chances are good that Alice is coming to you because she didn't get enough connected reading at her decoding level. Don't let her down!

Phase into regular connected reading.   As the payola phases out and Alice increases her accuracy, try this: "Now, Alice, you're doing so well I think you're ready to try this page without having me read it to you. Look it over first to see if there are any words you don't know."

If she messes it up, forget it for another day or week and go back to the reading model for each selection. In any case, provide the reading model some of the time each session.

When she begins to need the model less, she will soon be able to read silently. This means Alice has progressed to at least easy second-grade level and is ready to handle reading comprehension. Further guidelines to help you recognize when Alice is ready to decode *and* comprehend appear in the next section.

Comprehension

Listening Comprehension

At the beginning of Stage II, comprehension looks exactly like it did in late Stage I. Stick to listening comprehension until Alice has decoding down well enough to handle reading comprehension.

Listening comprehension means you will read to her and ask her questions about what she's heard. (See page 50 again for the main question types you can use.) *Caution:* Under no circumstances should you ask Alice questions about the connected reading while she's still working on perfect accuracy.

Reading Comprehension

There's really no big mystery about when to move from listening comprehension to reading comprehension. Alice will let you know she's ready by:

- forgetting the payola for perfect accuracy—this indicates she is beginning to concentrate more on what she's reading
- reading silently, that is, she can keep her place without saying the words orally (it's OK if she mouths the words softly)
- continuing to decode when you suddenly have to leave her (it's a good idea to plan a few fast getaways from time to time just to check this out)
- asking questions about what she is reading (this is the least efficient indicator since Alice may not want to make the reading session any longer than it has to be)

By the time all this takes place, Alice will be reading on at least a second-grade level, and the idea and vocabulary content of what she's reading will be somewhat more in keeping with her mental ability. For most older beginners, it's an insult to question them about first-grade materials.

In Stage I, I mentioned several types of questions you should ask Joe. There were vocabulary, recall, translation-sequencing, summary, inference, and critical-thinking questions (page 50). Here's how you would use these same questions during Stage II reading comprehension time:

- Select a very short story—five pages or less—that you know Alice could decode easily. Scan the pages quickly for words that Alice might not know. Besides asking her to pronounce a word, also ask her what the word means (vocabulary question). Don't overdo this. One word per page is more than enough.

- Have Alice read the whole story silently or quietly to herself. Leave her alone when she does this. (You might want to read the story yourself from another copy.)

- When Alice has finished decoding, take the book away from her and ask her to tell the story in her own words (translation-sequencing question). If she goes astray, keep after her by asking, "But what happened before that? . . . And then?" And so on.

- Give her back the book and, pointing to a page, present "find-it" problems, such as, "Read the part where it tells you what they did after the storm" (similar to a recall question except Alice finds the answer instead of remembering it). Then ask her to point to one sentence that tells what they did (summary question if she's just read you a paragraph).

- Take the book back and ask Alice about things that aren't there in black and white. "What time of the year do you think it was?" (Questions beginning with "Do you think" are usually inference questions.)

- As you're putting the book away, ask casually, "Could that story really have happened?" or "Do you think this is an old story?" (These are critical-thinking questions and inference questions.)

Like almost everything else in this book, the questions I've just suggested are guidelines. You don't have to go through the questions in the same order every time, nor do you really need to hit each type every session. You will soon know which types of questions give Alice the most trouble, and you'll probably spend most of your time on those.

Sometimes you may choose to go back to listening comprehension, and once in a while you may not touch comprehension at all. Don't feel guilty. You will get back to it when it feels right, and Alice will learn to comprehend what she reads.

Word-Attack Skills

Along with connected reading for accuracy, word-attack skills get top billing in Stage II. Not so strangely, they complement one another beautifully. If Alice is doing lots of connected reading at her decoding level, she is learning word-attack skills.

Which Word-Attack Skills Rate Four Stars?

Phonics is only one of several important word-attack skills. Two other skills of equal value are *structural analysis*—sort of a sight word approach to parts of words—and the use of *context*—figuring out an unknown word by using the known words around it. Spelling the word can also be helpful, at least on a temporary basis.

At Stage II it is important for Alice to:

- know letter names
- recognize the sounds of individual letters and blends
- blend separate sounds into a one-syllable word
- recognize common prefixes and suffixes on sight
- decode or recognize two or more separate syllables and blend them into a longer word
- be able to apply two rules—the rule of silent *e* and the rule for two different vowels side by side
- fill in missing words from context, that is, figure out unknown words on a page from the known words around it

That's it. Cut to their bare bones, the essentials of word attack are quite uncomplicated. You will become very familiar with them after studying the Word-Attack Skills Survey, on page 66.

What Word-Attack Skills Does Alice Know?

Use the Word-Attack Skills Survey (see page 66) with Alice early in Stage II to find out what she's missing. Try it again later in

Word-Attack Skills Survey

Part 1. *Directions:* Say the *names* of these letters.

k   t   o   f   b   e   s   v   q

a   l   r   n   c   p   g   u   i

Part 2. *Directions:* Say the *sounds* of these letters and groups of letters.

m   s   l   y   f   k   r   b   z

t   g   h   w   p   n   d   c   j

bl   fr   sn   ch   str

wh   sw   cl   scr   th

Part 3. *Directions:* What are these *nonsense* words? Figure them out.

sib   lem   dop   vac   nud

fets   ponning   hussed   wid's   tazzer

Part 4. *Directions:* Here are some more *nonsense* words. Figure them out.

siblem   doppet   widsud

disvacful   annertaz   contepness

Part 5. *Directions:* Here are some actual words. What are they? What is the rule that tells you how to pronounce the vowel sounds?

sale   lime   note   rude

Part 6. *Directions:* Here are some more actual words. What are they? What is the rule that tells you how to pronounce the vowel sounds?

road   main   peek   seal

Stage II to check on her progress. A blow-by-blow description of each part follows.

Scoring Guidelines

The following guidelines will help you to score Alice's survey. But before you score it, become familiar with it by doing Part 1 yourself, then studying the guidelines for Part 1, doing Part 2, then studying the guidelines for Part 2, and continuing in this way through all six parts. A score sheet with "Where-do-I-go-from-here?" ideas follows the guidelines.

Part 1. Knowing letter names.   This is a skill that is generally developed during Stage I. For some Alices it can serve as a bridge to the sounds of letters and blends—in other words, as a bridge to phonics. Other Alices seem to use letter names as a bridge to structural analysis, that is, after spelling *n–e–s–s* about 20 times they recognize it on sight as *ness*.

Part 2. Knowing the sounds of individual consonants and blends.   You probably didn't have much trouble understanding what this part was all about. Many people have lots of difficulty pronouncing these letter-sounds without a long *schwa* sound bringing up the rear (that is, *b* becomes *buh*). The idea is for Alice to get off the sound fast so that it may be blended quickly with the next sound. She may need to practice this until it becomes automatic. You'll see why when you consider Part 3 of this test. Certain consonant blends (*bl, scr,* etc.) should also become automatic. Note that some groups of letters actually have a different sound when they come together than when they appear singly (*ch,* for example, has a sound quite different from *c* and *h*).

Part 3. Being able to blend separate sounds into a one-syllable word or nonsense syllable.   The first line in Part 3 represents words that can be decoded by simple c-v-c (consonant-short vowel-consonant) attack. If in doubt, Alice should automatically use the most common short vowel sound (*red, clam*). About 75 percent of the time she'll be right, since c-v-c words with other vowel sounds, like *her* and *what,* are relatively rare. Nonsense words are used here so Alice can't rely on her sight vocabulary. She should pronounce the vowels on the survey as follows:

a in *vac* like *a* in *cat*

e in *lem* like *e* in *bed*

i in *sib* like *i* in *bib*

o in *dop* like *o* in *mop*

u in *nud* like *u* in *cup*

Note: If you and Alice live in Arkansas, chances are that you won't pronounce the word *pen* as these rules indicate, but as *pin.* As long as such variations are consistent, there's no problem. Correcting what is regionally or culturally a perfectly acceptable pronunciation is not necessary, and will only discourage Alice.

As you can readily see, figuring out each individual letter sound is a very elementary and slow way to attack words. If Alice had to work this hard at more than 1 word in 20, I guarantee you she would put the book down and head for the refrigerator. Fortunately she won't have to work out more than 1 word in 20 as long as she's on her decoding level.

The strange words in the second line in Part 3 are perfectly decodable if you combine the c-v-c attack described above with a few basic structural endings. Most Alices reading on second-grade level will have no problem with the endings, although the c-v-c attack they have to go through for the first part of the word will take longer. Fortunately the more Alice decodes, the more elements like prefixes and suffixes become part of her sight vocabulary. However, at Stage II reading you do need to point out some of them to Alice if they don't come naturally. The most common suffixes appropriate for Stage II are:

plurals—*s* and *es*

possessives—*'s* and *s'*

regular verb endings—*s, ed,* and *ing*

contractions—*n't*

adjective and adverb endings—*er, est,* and *ly*

All of these are easy since they are about 90 percent regular. For example, *ly* will always sound the same and come at the end of a word. Even better, Alice usually learns them through connected reading alone. *Can't* even has an apostrophe to hit you between the eyes. What's more, it's easy to recognize *wasn't, hadn't,* and scores of others after the first *can't.* Now there's utility for you!

Part 4. Decoding (recognizing) two or more syllables and blending them into a longer word. The nonsense words in the first line of this part are strictly phonetic and again follow the c-v-c approach. Actually it's c-v-c-/c-v-c with a blend where the slash is. For example, Alice will figure out *sib* and *lem* separately, then blend them together for *siblem.*

The second line consists of three-syllable nonsense words; however, some of the syllables are regular prefixes and suffixes that Alice will often know on sight. Most of our longer words do contain known prefixes and suffixes. (Lucky for us!)

In attacking longer words, Alice should learn to handle certain basic structural elements, including:

- compound words made from two known words (*snowball, whatever*)
- prefixes (*un, re*)
- suffixes (*ful, ness*)
- common stem or root words (*help, do*)
- inflectional forms (the verb, adjective, and adverb endings mentioned above in Part 3)

Part 5. Knowing and/or being able to apply the rule of silent e. Phonetic rules are very shaky, but there are two that hold up often enough in the face of irregularities to merit memorization, application, or both. This is one of them (the second is given in Part 6): A silent *e* at the end of a word makes the previous vowel long. Here it's important for Alice to know that long vowels are pronounced like their letter names. Otherwise the rule isn't going to do her much good, is it?

Part 6. Knowing and/or being able to apply the rule that when two vowels appear together, the first vowel is usually long and the second one silent. Sometimes this second rule is said this way: "When two vowels go walking, the first one does the talking." Now isn't that a gas! I've placed this rule last for a reason. It will hold true only 47 percent of the time. Consider: Even if Alice learns the rule and applies it, she has over a 50-50 chance of being wrong. There are always *oil, believe,* and a host of other nasty exceptions around. Most of the other phonics rules hold up even less than 47 percent of the time. (And so I'm not very impressed with them.)

Giving Alice the Survey

Now that you understand the survey and know what you're after, it's time to use it.

- Make two copies of the survey, one for Alice to work from and one for you to mark on.
- Go through the survey with Alice, checking or marking the items she misses. Don't help her. Hide your copy and make some kind of mark on the paper for every item, whether Alice is correct or incorrect. Otherwise Alice may tune in more to your marking than to the task.
- Stop the survey whenever Alice misses over half the items in a line. For example, if she messes up on *sib, lem,* and *dop* in the first line of Part 3, stop the survey. Parts 2 and 5, line by line, are listed in order of difficulty. If Alice can't do the first line of Part 3, she won't be able to do the second line.
- After the test, record Alice's scores on the Word-Attack Skills Survey Score Sheet (see page 71) and check the appropriate box—"OK" or "Needs Help."

Now when you give Alice this test and she does fine with a section—only misses one thing or none—for heaven's sweet sake, believe that she knows the skill in question! Alice doesn't need to know the rules if she can apply them! I'll never understand why some people put so much time and effort into page after page of exercises that are completely uncalled for, or, at best, are only partially appropriate. I would guess that it uses up more workbooks and keeps Alice off the streets, but if that's what you're after, the last thing you want is a survey. Better not to know that you're wasting Alice's time.

It certainly won't hurt, on the other hand, to give Alice some instruction on the two or more items she missed on a section. For

Word-Attack Skills Survey
Score Sheet

Name_____

Date_____

Part	Line(s)	Skill	Possible Score	Pupil's Score	OK*	Needs Help**
1	1, 2	letter names	18		(15-18)	(0-14)
2	1, 2	single consonant sounds	18		(15-18)	(0-14)
2	3, 4	consonant blends	10		(8-10)	(0-7)
3	1	c-v-c words	5		(4-5)	(0-3)
3	2	c-v-c/suffix words	5		(4-5)	(0-3)
4	1	c-v-c/c-v-c words	3		(2-3)	(0-1)
4	2	longer words	3		(2-3)	(0-1)
5	1	rule of silent *e*	4		(3-4)	(0-2)
6	1	rule for side-by-side vowels	4		(3-4)	(0-2)

*"OK" means that you may want to work on the few items missed, but the skill is basically there.

**"Needs Help" means the skill isn't there and needs quite a bit of work. See page 73 for a guide to the basic exercises to use.

example, it is not uncommon for someone to miss only *w* and *j* out of the isolated letter-sounds.

And here's another earthshaker. The phonics presented on the Word-Attack Skills Survey are all you need to know—ever—period—end of report. With these skills in hand, plus context and lots of practice with connected reading, Alice will keep raising her reading level. The sky's the limit.

Generally anyone who can decode a third-grade book will do well on the Word-Attack Skills Survey and vice versa. The only things that could possibly keep Alice from decoding at third-grade level if she has these skills are (1) lack of sight vocabulary— particularly basic utility words, and (2) lack of practice in connected reading (can't keep her place for beans, for example). If your Alice is like that, do more work on sight vocabulary and connected reading! Save the following basic exercises for an Alice who needs them.

Basic Exercises in Word Attack

You've completed the Word-Attack Skills Survey Score Sheet so you know which skills Alice needs help with—they were the ones you checked in the "Needs Help" column. On the following pages are exercises you can use to help her. Find the ones which will help Alice by using the table on page 73.

Sounds of Letters in Pictures

This exercise will help Alice to distinguish:
 • single consonant sounds
For the exercise you will need:
 • letter cards
 • old magazines
 • scissors
 • construction paper and paste (optional)
 • ready-made picture cards (optional)
Give Alice a letter *b* card and a magazine. Go over the sound of the letter with her. Have her cut out pictures of things that start

Skill	Exercises	Page
letter names	Recognition and Tracking	41
single consonant sounds	Sounds of Letters in Pictures Sounds of Word Parts in Print	72 74
consonant blends	Sounds of Word Parts in Print c-v-c Practice with Words	74 76
c-v-c words	Vowel Recognition and Short Vowel Sounds c-v-c Practice with Words c-v-c Games	74 76 79
c-v-c/suffix words	Syllables and Such	81
c-v-c/c-v-c and longer words	Syllables and Such	81
rule of silent *e* and rule for side-by-side vowels	Sounds of Word Parts in Print Vowel Rules	74 80

with the *b* sound (biscuits, barrels, batteries). She may paste them on construction paper if you're both willing. Tackle a different sound every day. This very common activity is usually given much too early—often at the kindergarten level. Actually the picture finding is often harder for a person who has trouble distinguishing sounds (an auditory discrimination problem) than the game "I'm going on a trip." The pictures may distract Alice from concentrating on the sounds. Also, matching pictures to letter sounds involves sight-sound association.

Variation 1.   A helpful variation is to have Alice select pictures of things that end in a particular sound (phone, button, corn). Don't worry about the ending *letter* or letters (like the silent *e* in phone), so long as the ending *sound* is correct.

Variation 2.   If the cut-and-paste routine seems a bit tacky—and it well may if Alice is over third-grade age—you can give her ready-cut pictures on cards to sort. You can buy sets of picture cards for this purpose or, if you have some of those phonics workbooks hanging around, you can cut them up and make your own. This will make phonics readiness more palatable for the older Alice, and you can select only those sounds that she needs to work on.

Variation 3.   If Alice is having trouble with letter sounds, part of your session should include the listening exercises you used with Joe, like "I'm going to Java and I'm going to take a man and a pan. What will you take?" (see page 47).

Sounds of Word Parts in Print

Here Alice will learn:
  • letter names
  • single consonant sounds
  • consonant blends
  • short vowel sounds
  • prefixes
  • suffixes
  • rule of silent *e*
  • rule for side-by-side vowels
You will need:
  • pages of print
  • a marking pen or pencil

Pick a word-attack element (single letter-sound, blend, prefix, or suffix) that gave Alice difficulty on her survey. Give her a page of print and a card with the element on it (like *str, w,* or *ly*). Have her track line by line on the page, marking the element each time it appears and making the appropriate sound as she marks it.

Vowel Recognition and Short Vowel Sounds

In this exercise Alice will learn to recognize:
  • vowels in general
  • short vowel sounds in print

Sounds of Word Parts in Print

$\breve{i}$	Short $\underline{i}$

X ⟶
This is just like the first recognition and tracking exercise you did with Joe. You can use it for short vowel sounds and lots of other things.

You will need:

- handmade vowel charts showing *a, e, i, o,* and *u* (*y* comes later)
- individual vowel cards as needed to practice short vowel sounds
- an alphabet strip or sheet
- letter cards or tiles
- pages of print
- a marking pen or pencil

First make sure Alice can recognize all the vowels without fail. Use the letter tiles and handmade vowel chart, and spend one day on "Which letters are the vowels?" Alice uses the vowel chart as a guide and checks through the letter tiles to find the vowels. When she finds a vowel, she puts the letter tile under the same vowel on the alphabet strip.

To reinforce Alice's recognition of vowels and to make her conscious of how they appear in words, repeat the marking-in-print exercise asking Alice to look for and circle all the vowels as she goes. But don't have Alice pronounce what she's marking this time, since some of the vowels will be silent.

If the survey has left any doubt remaining as to whether Alice knows the basic short sounds of the vowels, make up some picture-letter cards like those teachers use to teach the short vowel sounds initially—for example, a card showing both a picture of a cat, and the word cat with the *a* underlined. Work with these until when you show Alice an *a* letter tile and ask "What sound does this usually make?" you get the short *a* sound pronto.

Vowel Recognition and Short Vowel Sounds in Print

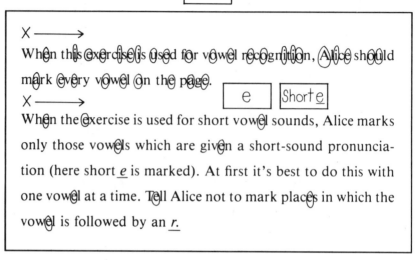

Important: Wean Alice from such cards before you start c-v-c practice. The response must be *automatic* and that means that the learning devices are no longer needed.

Perhaps after more c-v-c work with some of the exercises that follow, try Alice with the pages of print. Give her one short vowel sound to look for, remind her that she's looking "for all the places you see an *e* (eh) sound," and turn her loose with the marking pen.

c-v-c Practice with Words

Alice will work with:
- c-v-c word attack
- consonant blends

You will need:
- word cards of typical c-v-c words
- handmade worksheets (see the sample below)
- letter cards or tiles
- a marking pen or pencil

Show Alice several c-v-c word cards that feature the same short vowel (*bad, cab, man, sat*). Give her a worksheet like the one below and a whole batch of consonant letter tiles. Tell her to reconstruct the words on the chart. Be sure to use big *a*'s and big spaces so the letter tiles will fit.

c-v-c Practice with Words Using Letter Tiles

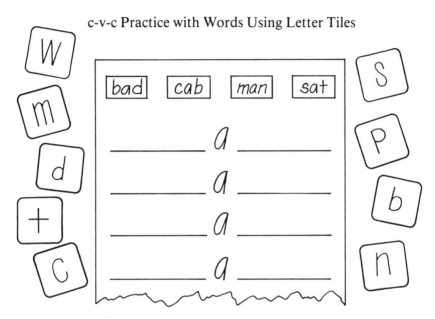

When she has finished the words you gave her, have her try making some of her own. Talk about the words, having Alice *un*blend them. (For example, have her say *bad* in three separate sounds: *b–a–d*.)

You will eventually work on all the short vowels this way. Tomorrow's word group may be *pen, set, bed,* and *wet,* and all the words Alice can develop on her own. Just be sure short *a* is down pat before you move on to short *e*, and so forth.

Sooner or later you will need to include consonant blends before and after the short vowel. This is really pretty easy for Alice if she knows such blends as *ch, bl, ck,* and *str.* Consonant blend words follow the basic c-v-c pattern in words such as *chat, black,* and *string. Caution:* You and Alice can hardly mess up on this unless you use *r* at the end of the word. The letter *r* does strange things to the vowel it follows (*star, her, fir, for,* and *blur*).

For now, just outlaw *r* at the end of a c-v-c word. Chances are excellent that Alice will pick up "*r*-controlled vowels" on her own as she practices decoding. If she doesn't, you can work on it later. Right now she doesn't need exceptions to the rule she's trying to learn.

Variation 1. Reduce the size of the letters and blanks on a worksheet like the one below and have Alice write consonants or consonant blends in the blanks. Always have her read the words she makes and unblend them for you. *Caution:* The letter *r* at the end is still forbidden.

Variation 1: Sheet for c-v-c Practice with Words

_____ a _____	_____ a _____
_____ a _____	_____ a _____
_____ a _____	_____ a _____
_____ a _____	_____ a _____
_____ a _____	_____ a _____
_____ a _____	_____ a _____
_____ a _____	_____ a _____

Variation 2. This time give Alice a few nonsense words similar to the ones on the survey (*sib, lim, nid*). Have her say them and write them on a worksheet like the one used in Variation 1 above. Now let her loose creating more nonsense words.

Variation 3. Collect all the papers Alice has completed for c-v-c practice. Give her a blank piece of paper and a pencil. Have Alice write about 20 c-v-c's from dictation. Use real and nonsense c-v-c's picked at random.

c-v-c *Games*

Alice will work on:
- recognizing vowels
- c-v-c word attack

You will need:
- letter cards or tiles
- a Scrabble board
- handmade bingo cards
- handmade dice
- other games

Games are a big part of c-v-c practice. Most of them are already known to Alice.

Scrabble.　Dust off the Scrabble board and play a game using c-v-c words. Scrabble even comes with its own letter tiles.

Bingo.　If Scrabble is too hard, make a set of bingo cards like the ones shown.

Vowel-Practice Bingo Cards

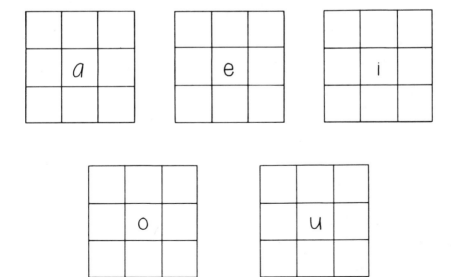

Give Alice the bingo card for the vowel of the day. Mix up a pile of consonant letter tiles (with *r* removed, of course). Pick a letter tile and call it out. Have Alice write it down anywhere on her card, or just hand her the tile to place on the card. Do this until all the squares are full. Give her a point for every c-v-c word she can decode, real and nonsense words alike. Let her read in any direction. This can be a dandy group game, too.

Roll the dice.   In Las Vegas, where I live, it's easy to get blank dice. (It isn't so easy to mark on them, however!) If you don't live in Las Vegas and you can't obtain blank dice anywhere, you might try using the smallest wooden blocks you can find (although these are quite a handful even then). Put a vowel on each face of one die. (You'll need to repeat one vowel.) Mark two other dice with an assortment of consonants or consonant blends on their faces. Your finished set will look something like the ones shown here.

Phonics Practice Dice

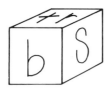 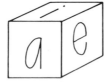 

Roll 'em and say 'em!

There are lots of games like these on the market. Visit your local school supply house or that section of your bookstore, and shop around.

Vowel Rules

Alice will learn:

- long vowels
- rule of silent *e*
- rule for side-by-side vowels

You will need:

- a handmade long vowel chart
- word cards
- pages of print
- a marking pen or pencil

Rule of silent e. This skill is taught directly. Explain to Alice that most of the time vowels have their most common short sound, but sometimes they have a long sound.

A long vowel sound is just like its letter name. Present the chart and name the letter: *a, e, i, o, u.* Explain that very often when there's an *e* on the end of a word, that *e* is silent. And that silent *e* usually makes the vowel before it long.

Take out Alice's sight vocabulary cards and look for *e*'s at the end of words (*make, like, cone*). Ask Alice, "Is the *e* silent? Does it make the vowel before it long?" (Be careful what you choose. There are a lot of exceptions, such as *have, give, live, shove* that you can point out later.) Go on to pages of print, having Alice mark final *e*'s and determine whether the preceding vowel is long.

The rule of silent *e* is usually very easy to learn. If Alice has mastered c-v-c words using short vowels, you can expect her to catch on to this rule in one or two sessions. If she hasn't mastered c-v-c, you shouldn't be doing this yet anyway!

Rule for side-by-side vowels. You might not want to fool with this rule at all, since there are just as many exceptions as there are regular examples. If Alice is easily confused and frustrated, just skip it. Go over a page of print that Alice has been reading and see for yourself if there are more words like *keep, coast,* and *suit* (regular) or more like *look, bread,* and *laugh* (exceptions). If you decide to proceed, go ahead just the way you did for the rule of silent *e* above.

Syllables and Such

Alice will work on:

- just about everything she has done to date, plus compound words and blending syllables

You will need:

- word cards (any with two or more syllables that Alice has in her sight vocabulary)
- pages of print
- a marking pen or pencil
- a spelling dictionary

Start out by treating yourself to a spelling dictionary. This is a handy little book of words without definitions—just the correct spelling and syllable breaks. You'll find that it's a lot easier to locate a word and decipher the markings in this dictionary than in a standard dictionary. For example, the spelling dictionary uses only three marks: a dot, a heavy accent mark, and a lighter accent mark. Every syllable has one of the three marks setting it off.

Use the spelling dictionary to divide the words on Alice's word cards. First find the word for Alice in the dictionary. Then have Alice copy it exactly as it appears (*a. wake, in· vi· ta'· tion*). Explain that each part is pronounced separately and has at least one vowel. The parts may be called out in order if Alice knows them on sight; if she doesn't know a part she can sound it out. (She probably knows the parts since they were on her word cards.)

Now get rid of the cards and have Alice say *awake*. Ask her how many word parts she hears. How about *invitation*? If, after all that, Alice can't hear the separate syllables, exaggerate them by unblending them for her (*in–vi–ta–tion*). If she still doesn't get the idea, continue to work orally until she can unblend known words herself.

If she could tell you how many parts there are in *awake* and *invitation,* work with the rest of her word cards in the following steps:

- Read the word to Alice.
- Have her tell you how many parts are in the word.
- Write the word on paper.
- Have Alice use dots to separate the word into syllables (use dots even where accent marks would appear).
- Check the word in the spelling dictionary—you find the word, but have Alice check her work.

Variation 1.   Use pages of print with at least some words of two or more syllables. Have Alice track through the page (just as she did in "Sounds of Word Parts in Print") to find them. Then have her try to decode the shorter ones.

Variation 2.   If Variation 1 is too difficult, copy the words that Alice finds, separating them into syllables. (I told you that a spelling dictionary would come in handy!) Then have Alice try decoding the parts in order.

A Final Word About Phonics and Structural Analysis

The proof of the skills comes out during connected reading when Alice decodes new words by herself, within 5 seconds, without any help. If you still have to remind her what to do, she hasn't mastered the skill. Don't remind her during connected reading, but make a mental note, or a written one, to take up the missing skill during word-attack time.

Context Exercises

One of the most useful word-attack skills known is the use of context—the words around the word you're trying to understand. I guarantee you use it all the time—without it you would have stayed at third-grade reading level.

The only way you can learn to use context is through connected reading. Words in isolation just won't do the job. When Alice is unable to use context, your first guess is that most of her reading instruction has been with isolated sight vocabulary and phonics. Another good guess is that the way she strings words together when she talks is different from the way the writer does it in the material she's trying to read. Modeling should definitely help in the latter case, but you can't beat encouraging Alice to try using context clues.

Listening for Context Clues

The general idea.   Read to Alice without letting her look at the material. Stop every so often and ask Alice what she thinks will happen next. You might notice that this is also a part of listening comprehension. If you don't get any response, say, "Well, I think such-and-so will happen because. . . ." Explain how you arrived at your conclusion.

Specific words.   Explain to Alice that while you are reading to her you are going to stop somewhere in each sentence. She is to supply the next word; then you will finish the sentence. Use a story for this. The material can be harder than her connected reading material since Alice will not be looking at the printed page. If she picks a word or words other than the ones in the sentence (and that could happen quite often), say, "Good, that's a lot like what's written here." Reread the whole sentence before continuing.

If she has trouble, pick a story she already knows, like "The Three Little Pigs." At the very least, stick to a subject she can talk about intelligently. Stop on obvious words when you start to work with context clue reading: "I'll huff and I'll puff and I'll _____ your house down."

Extra practice.   Straight vocabulary study is a great help in getting words from context clues. For example, say, "I'm thinking of a word that means the same as *smart*. It starts with a *b* (letter or sound, whichever she's using now). . . . No, it's longer than *bright*. . . . Yes, it's *brilliant*." This one's a lot harder than the others, so be wary of it if Alice doesn't have a pretty good speaking vocabulary.

Context with Printed Material

The general idea.   Simply transpose the first exercise above to the printed page. Let Alice follow along in the book, stopping and covering up the rest of the page from time to time so she can respond to "What do you think will happen next?" (With a group, have them close their books with a finger in the place.)

Specific words.   Now transpose the second exercise above to the printed page. This time the reading selection does have to be on Alice's decoding level because she will read along and supply the missing word. You will need a photocopy and a big bottle of white typing correction fluid. Take the photocopy and white out key words (like *blow* in the "huff and puff" example above). What you produce will look like the Sample Context Exercise. Some people have better luck using a big black marking pen. Whatever you do, get rid of the words you want Alice to supply. If there's even a trace left, she's likely to spend more time looking at that trace than thinking about what would fit in.

Sample Context Exercise

It's a good idea to leave at least 10 or _____ words between blanks. (This isn't supposed to be at frustration _____.) On the other hand, if a word is distinctive you don't have to _____ for the tenth word. When Alice is finished have her _____ the whole exercise aloud.

Don't correct Alice unless her fill-ins are completely off base. If they are, try material that is easier, material that she knows more about, or do more modeling of connected reading.

Variation. This variation is closer to what really happens when Alice reads. White out some of the key words but leave certain telltale evidence behind—an initial consonant blend here, a suffix there. If you didn't make it to the copying machine, you can put your finger over a word every so often, or maybe use a word-sized piece of cardboard. The variation isn't as helpful as the white-out version since you're bound to cover up more than just one word. It's certainly better than nothing, though, and you needn't apologize for it.

Cloze technique. For the more advanced Stage II reader (one who can almost read a third-grade book), you can use a standard cloze technique. *Cloze* is just a sophisticated term for what's been going on in these exercises—supplying a missing word by looking at those that are present. (Some day someone may ask, "Have you tried the cloze technique?" and you'll say "Sure!")

Type out a selection at Alice's decoding level on a large print typewriter, or do it by hand in manuscript. One page is plenty to start—you can work up to two or even three pages for more advanced readers. Make two complete copies of the selection. On one copy white out every tenth word, twelfth word, or whatever so you have something that looks like the Sample Cloze Selection shown. Be consistent. If you can, draw a line under the space where the word is to go. (This isn't absolutely necessary, but it does make some Alices feel more secure.)

Sample Cloze Selection

> Type out a selection at Alice's decoding level _____ a large print typewriter, or do it by_____ in manuscript. One page is plenty to start—you can _____ up to two or even three pages for more _____ readers. Make two complete copies. On one _____ white out every tenth word, twelfth word,_____ whatever. Be consistent. If you can, draw a _____ under the space where the word is _____ go.

Give Alice the copy with the blanks. Have her fill in the blanks. When she has finished, give her the original copy and either have her correct her work alone or work with her. This procedure is known to do just about everything but teach her to ski. For now we'll concentrate simply on its value in teaching her to use context clues, and indirectly for increasing her confidence. (You may well wonder about the latter. Give her the next page of her reading selection without any white outs, watch her attack it with gusto, and you'll see what I mean. She knows now that she can make sense out of material in which some of the words are missing, so it seems easy to read a passage that's complete.)

Writing as a Reading Exercise

Up to this point I haven't mentioned much about the benefits of writing in mastering word-attack skills. You may recall it was discussed under learning words in Stage I as a possible "when-all-else-fails" approach. The Stage II reader, on the other hand, will have had more experience with written work. Unless Alice still finds it so difficult to make letters that she can't think about anything else, writing words is a great device to help teach reading. The technique is called *overlearning* and it's what happens when you already know something but you keep working on it to make sure that you won't forget it. You need to drop down to a very easy decoding level for the greatest benefit. Working at independent level is best.

Have Alice write sentences from dictation. The best sentences will contain words in her sight vocabulary. She can study the sentence first, then write it from dictation. This is a prime overlearning experience for reading, and it's bound to improve the way Alice writes, too. It's particularly helpful if Alice is one of those hard-core reluctant readers who forgets too many words. Writing will help cement them.

How Alice Graduates to Stage III

When Alice can decode most of the unfamiliar words she encounters within 5 seconds each, she is ready for Stage III. By that time she will be able to do all the tasks in the Word-Attack Skills Survey. This usually means that Alice can also decode easy third-grade material—that is, she will miss no more than 1 word in 20 in an easy third-grade book. (You can check this with Sample B of the Decoding Level Survey, page 13.)

Ideally Alice will no longer stumble on basic utility words and she will be able to answer questions correctly about what she reads. These skills are nice, but the lack of them is no grounds for holding her back in Stage II.

Is She Really Ready?

Let's say you've put in 100 sessions, or 50 hours, and Alice still needs to work on most of the Word-Attack Skills Survey items. Three factors exist that will influence advanced placement:

- the size of her sight vocabulary (can she almost handle that easy third-grade material with sight words alone?)
- how well she uses context clues (does she consistently correct herself after she's completed a sentence?)
- her age (is she over 13?)

If the answers to two of the three questions are yes, graduate her to Stage III. The emphasis on developing word-attack skills is different in Stage III and quite possibly is just what Alice needs.

If Alice is over 13 but falls short in the sight vocabulary and context clues departments, continue in Stage II; however, try different reading materials and move slowly on the word-attack skills. Repeat an exercise several times before moving on to the next one. After another 25 or so sessions, by all means move her into Stage III regardless of her readiness. Nothing ventured, nothing gained.

Helping Danny, A Stage III Reader

Danny is 14—but he could be as young as 11 or as old as 81. Danny is almost functionally literate. On a good day he can read third-grade or even fourth-grade material at decoding level. Whether he comprehends it may be an entirely different story, as we shall see.

Danny attacks an oral reading situation with a good deal of bravado. He picks up a book masterfully, clears his throat, and begins the first sentence in a strong voice. Before he utters a dozen words, however, he has repeated the sentence twice and given you at least one plausible reason for why he did this. When you do not seem eager to be sidetracked, he slouches a bit, lets the book slip down on the table, and lowers his voice several decibels. What follows is a painful recital filled with hesitations, repetitions, some messing up of simple words, and no phrasing to speak of. This is the first and most common characteristic of the Stage III reader—a decoding level of third or fourth grade, but a performance that is rapid, halting, or painful. Your reaction is, "Simmer down, pal, and smooth it out!"

You'll also notice the next most common characteristic of a Stage III reader during an oral reading performance. Danny generally has a big stock of excuses and gimmicks to get him out of the reading situation and into talking with you. After all, he's had a longer time to develop them than a Stage II reader—and survival in high school and the world has depended upon getting out of reading. Small wonder Danny is so good at it. If he doesn't try to get out of reading, I'd worry about him. This could mean he's given up on himself as well as on reading.

It goes without saying that Danny is firmly convinced he will never be able to read well. His feeling of inferiority is in fact your biggest stumbling block. At best he will come in disposed to tolerate the instruction and cooperate with you. But down deep he knows these reading sessions are going to take him exactly where all those other tutoring situations and remedial classes did—nowhere!

A rather surprising characteristic of the Stage III reader, you may think, is that he or she is likely to do quite well on the Word-Attack Skills Survey (page 66). Actually it shouldn't be all that surprising, since I told you before that anyone who can decode on easy third-grade level will know these skills or, more importantly, be able to apply them.

Danny's comprehension may be anywhere until he gets used to you. Comprehension requires concentration. You can bet Danny is thinking more about what you're going to have him do than what the book says. There are exceptions. Some Stage III readers concentrate mainly on trying to understand what they read, even if they can't figure out a lot of the words. You're really in luck if your problem reader is inclined this way! It's much easier to increase Danny's decoding ease and speed than to build comprehension skills. Then again, increasing comprehension is not that tough. You'll be a pro at it after digesting this chapter. You'll get to use your new skills too, because you can bet that Danny will have reading comprehension problems with ninth-grade material, since he's never been able to decode it. Danny won't write well either. His penmanship may be fantastic, but you can bet his spelling won't be.

What Danny's Job Is

Danny's number 1 job is to survive high school or the adult world in spite of his reading level. Make no mistake about it—that's number 1. His second job is to make the most of what he has, and gain confidence enough to do this. Danny probably believes that since he can't decode his schoolbooks, it's useless to try any reading. (An amazing number of Stage III readers seem to shoot up several grade levels in as many weeks, which just goes to show you how important practice can be.) His third job is to improve his decoding rate and comprehension as quickly as possible.

What Your Job Is

You are to help Danny survive in high school (or society), make the most of what he has, and increase his decoding rate and comprehension. Don't snicker—believe it! At no other stage is the teacher, parent, tutor, or friend more important than in this one. You may be the only life raft in sight. You can *save Danny from a lifetime of illiteracy.*

Starting Out with an Older Problem Reader

When you work with Danny, you are not going to fall into several old traps that have led to his failure in the past. First, you are not going to do something for Danny, he's going to do it for himself. You're there to make it possible. For this reason you are not going to reach for a canned program guaranteed to teach older problem readers how to read better, because that program can't do it for him either. I repeat, Danny has to do it for himself.

You are not going to play games with Danny. You're going to tell him his strengths and his weaknesses as concretely as possible, and explain exactly how he can use them, strengthen them, or avoid them. Danny must begin to think of himself as a worthwhile person who is capable of making his own learning decisions. You are there to help him do what he decides. Of course, you can present your case.

Find Out More About His Reading

What's Danny's silent reading like? Go back to Sample B in the Decoding Level Survey (page 13). Have Danny read this silently, keeping track of how long it takes him to finish the passage. Don't set a stopwatch, but keep track with the second hand on a watch. One minute is good. Two minutes is OK (not good, just OK). Three minutes is slow (about what you might expect). Four minutes is very slow, and five or more minutes is like cold molasses. Don't comment now, however. Put the paper out of sight and ask Danny questions like the following:

- "What was the girl's (woman's) name?" (Lisa)
- "Who had a new car?" (Sam, or the cousin, or the guy who was visiting them)
- "Where were they going?" (to the lake)
- "Why wasn't Sam worried about police cars?" (because he had a CB)
- "How did the police find them?" (CB, or radar, or speed trap, or hiding behind the hill)

If Danny answers all five questions correctly, his comprehension is good on that decoding level. Four correct answers is OK. But only three right answers is not OK, and you'll really have to work on comprehension. If Danny can't even answer three questions, I'd assume that he is still too uptight with the situation to give you an accurate estimate. Try the same exercise using different materials when you get to know one another better. Hold off for now.

What Word-Attack Skills Does He Have?

If your Danny is 13 or under, you might want to try the Word-Attack Skills Survey from Stage II (page 66). An 11-year-old Danny has more time to polish up isolated skills than a Danny who is 14 or 21 years old—at least three years more. The Word-Attack Skills Survey is optional for pupils who could accurately decode Sample B on the Decoding Level Survey. Danny couldn't have decoded Sample B without having those word-attack skills, anyway.

Level with Danny

Let's assume that your typical 14-year-old Danny performed like this: His oral reading of Sample B was jerky, halting, and painful, but he missed no more than 5 words (his decoding level is easy third grade or better). Three days later you had him read the same sample silently and answer questions. He did it in 3 minutes (slow) and answered four questions correctly (comprehension OK).

Now you're ready to level with Danny. For example, tell him that his word-attack skills are basically OK, and that as far as you're concerned he'll never get any phonics exercises from you. Usually this gets his attention better than a 2-by-4 across the skull. Say something like, "You seem to understand what you read fairly well. Of course, this page isn't as hard as the ones you're probably used to."

Then get to the heart of the matter. "Your reading aloud (stress *aloud*) is pretty slow and choppy. The page you read was on about a third-grade level. Your silent reading is slow, but probably on a higher level. That's what we should work on since you'll be using silent reading more." Now, for sure, you have his attention. By this time he's thinking, "What kind of tutoring is this? No phonics worksheets and no reading out loud?"

You plunge the hook in a little deeper: "I can show you how to read faster and better, so you can get your reading assignments done on time." (Or, ". . . so you can read the sports page in 10 minutes.")

Listen to Danny

About now Danny should be relaxed enough to tell you how he's surviving in school or society. Here's where you need to put aside your last remnants of Puritan ethics and really listen to him. You may hear how he uses tricks to get out of oral reading in class, how he cuts classes so he won't have to face a teacher without his homework, how he copies a good friend's notebook, how he gets this smart girl to write his term papers, how he cheats on his tests. (Does it sound like I've been there?) If Danny is older you may hear how he calls information rather than look up a telephone number, takes the job application home for his sister to fill out for him, memorizes the TV schedule from viewing, says he broke his glasses so his employer will read the safety bulletin to him, has his girl friend order at the restaurant. What you need to do is keep your eye on the doughnut instead of the hole. He's using these tricks to survive because up to now there has been no other avenue open to him. He cannot do ninth-grade reading and writing activities with a third-grade reading level. Adult literacy calls for a fifth-grade to sixth-grade reading level. Be glad he's trying to survive.

The Hard Sell

If he isn't trying to survive—that is, if he has already dropped out in spirit if not in body—your job is much tougher and requires a harder sell or a different approach. For example, his being with you, supposedly working on reading, may be just a trick to get you off his back. If he shows no interest in attempting to learn, deal the cards like this: "OK, you're going to be here for an hour twice a week. Maybe you've got better things to do and maybe I have, but we're stuck with each other. We have to work on reading, but nobody is going to tell us how or what to read. Next time bring in something you want me to read to you. I don't care what it is, so long as it's not x-rated. If you forget, I'll have something." (You guessed it—it's going to be "reading model" time.)

If he's just wishy-washy about the whole thing, it's hard-sell time. Start by telling Danny that if he wants to read better and is willing to practice the things you suggest, he will notice a big difference in *four* weeks—like possibly increasing his reading level two grades. That just might arouse his attention to the point that he'll ask you what he'll have to do. And this show of interest is what you're after.

Show him what the reading model thing is all about, and give him a sample of the kinds of comprehension exercises you would recommend. (Don't panic—you *are* going to read the rest of this chapter before you see Danny, aren't you?) Do this with Danny whether he's the same Danny we started out with, the wishy-washy one above, or the captive-audience Danny who is now tired of having you read the driver's manual or *Cycle World* to him. Sooner (you hope) or maybe later, you're after a commitment: "You agree to practice reading a half-hour every day with me or the tape recorder. Therefore by February you will be able to read a chapter in your health book (or a story in *Sports Illustrated*) in 30 minutes without any help." This sounds like a formal contract and it very well may be. Of course, many Dannys are willing to take any sort of promised improvement on faith. But you can't blame them if they won't. It won't hurt you to set a specific goal or two, either.

Help Outside the Reading Sessions

Typing Class

The very first thing I'd try to do after setting the stage is get Danny thinking about signing up to learn typing as soon as possible. "Personal Typing" is fine—you're not preparing him to be a secretary. Typing does amazing things for many Dannys. It helps them with written expression, spelling, penmanship, and reading. Now where else can you get a bargain like that? And it doesn't even have one of those dreaded remedial labels on it! If I were Danny's parents I would do more than try to talk him into it. I'd get myself an appointment with the dean or counselor and work it into his schedule for sure.

There are several reasons why typing works so well with so many. First of all, typing is a legitimate subject—there's no stigma, so Danny is likely to approach it with an open mind. Second, it's action oriented—you're doing something with your hands at least. The vast majority of 14-year-old Dannys would rather be doing something "hands-on" than just sitting. So would many adults.

Now the language-learning aspects. There's plenty of built-in repetition of words, words, and more words to look at (and to hear, if tapes are used). There are automatic movement patterns with the fingers that help Danny remember the sequence of letters in words for both reading and spelling. As a special bonus, Danny's hand muscles will get stronger, so his handwriting will be easier to read. Research will back me up on this one.

Trying to teach Danny typing on your own will not be as beneficial as class instruction, simply because you won't be as regulated or able to spend as much time on it. Let the public schools do it, or suggest that Danny sign up for a class at night.

Somebody's Going to Have to Read to Him

Until Danny can handle the reading material independently, he has five choices for dealing with it: He's either going to have to hear it, work around it, cheat, drop out, or fail. It may be a comfort to some to know that Danny is not goldbricking after all—he really can't read. Unfortunately many people who work with older Dannys seem to believe that "hear it" and "cheat" are the same thing. Why is reading to Danny considered subversive, while dropping out or failing is believed to be part of life? Beats me, but there it is.

In Stages I and II you learned that comprehension is built first by listening. It's criminal to confine an otherwise bright Danny to his decoding level when he's capable of working with ideas four to five grades higher! It's quite probable that many blind youngsters get a better education than our problem readers—where the handicap is obvious we just work around it. Danny looks just like everybody else, so his handicap is overlooked. It's not considered subversive to read to the blind—but to Danny?

One word of caution here. The longer Danny has been experiencing a reading problem, the more likely it is that he will have initial difficulty in listening comprehension on his age level. If he responds with a glassy stare the first few times you read to him, tell him in your own words what the material means after you read it. You have to overcome years of confusion, and Danny may assume at first that he can't understand anything.

Danny is coming to you because he can't handle reading tasks assigned by the school or society. While it's not hard to figure out what teen-aged Danny needs to have read to him, essential material for adult Danny may take more thought. If in doubt, you can always rely on debts and taxes. Installment contracts and driver's test booklets are assigned by society just as surely as tomorrow's biology assignment is assigned by the school. When you read assignments to Danny, follow along with your finger and insist that he read silently as you read orally. That's the deal: "No follow along—no read." (There's that reading model approach again.) Even though the material is on frustration level (that's why you will never have him read orally unless he volunteers—fat chance!), he will gain in reading accuracy from it. Sooner than you can imagine he will be able to read some of it for himself. And one fine day he'll be able to handle his own reading assignments— all of them!

I realize that this is awfully hard to swallow, but it does work. I have living proof in my own home—two teen-agers with entirely different initial reading problems who now have added the final option, "read it myself," to the other four: hear it, work around it, drop out, or fail.

What Your Reading Sessions Will Be Like

Since the major areas for instruction are connected reading and comprehension, the time will be split between them equally. If your Danny is 12 years old or younger, your sessions will be like this:

15 minutes	15 minutes
Connected Reading	Comprehension Study Skills

The older Danny's session, however, will be slightly different. For him you will include two newcomers to the scene: survival skills and writing.

5 minutes	10 minutes	10 minutes	5 minutes
Survival Skills	Connected Reading	Comprehension Study Skills	Writing

There is nothing magical about the specific time allotments on the charts. If Danny is doing fine one day on connected reading, he might spend the entire time on that. Another time the whole session might be spent on comprehension and study skills. The idea is to give equal billing to connected reading and comprehension and study skills, not to establish lock-step time schedules.

There is a widespread theory that the problem reader in the upper age brackets must receive individual tutoring. Supposedly, the older Danny is just too upset about his low performance to do anything with his peers around. In practice we have found that many older problem readers actually seem to do better in small groups (no more than four). Perhaps it's the old "misery loves company" routine, or, more likely, that Danny is relieved at seeing others as bad off as he is.

It was fairly easy for you to estimate how long Stage I and Stage II would continue. After 30 sessions or 100 sessions, Joe and Alice would be able to do the following things, blip, blip, blip. Then they went on to the next stage. But how do you graduate from Stage III? Simple: You never really do. Danny practices connected reading, modeled and silent, and his ease and speed increase. As long as he keeps practicing, be it 6 months or 6 years, he will continue to gain. The sky's the limit. Comprehension is like that too. Thinking about what you're reading and doing something about it aren't things you put a ceiling on. The longer you do it, the better you get.

It's more realistic to question when *you* will get out of Danny's Stage III. You'll step out when:

- He appears confident enough to handle most of the reading assigned to him by the school or society.

- He is able to make progress on his own, that is, he can and will read silently and react appropriately to what he has read.

This does not happen overnight. Gradually encourage Danny to do more silent reading. By the time he's ready to fly on his own, even your tutoring sessions will consist largely of Danny reading silently to himself.

Survival Skills

The time you spend on survival skills is essentially a rap session with Danny. Put this at the beginning of each session because (1) it's extremely important, and (2) it usually starts the session on a positive note. (Remember, Danny would rather talk.)

Your major purpose in each survival skills time is to accentuate and reinforce the positive—this will help Danny put his best foot forward in school or society. Concentrate particularly on areas other than oral reading and reading comprehension where Danny may already shine or at least be average. These could be activities such as listening, asking questions, acting like a student or responsible employee, and turning in work.

Listening

Convince Danny that he is a good listener and that he can gain a great deal by being one. (During comprehension time you will make sure of this!) Not only does Danny have to think of himself as a good listener, he has to be convinced he is one of the best. You are replacing the old negative thought, "I'm a terrible reader," with the positive one, "I'm a great listener." (This comes to you courtesy of *Psychocybernetics,** which is must reading for anyone who wants to exchange negative images for positive ones. It even comes on tape, if you're interested.)

Asking Questions

Danny has a right to learn. If he can't gain much from the printed page, he has every right to hear the material and ask questions about it, just as the able reader will ask questions silently and

---

*Maxwell Maltz, *Psychocybernetics* (New York: Prentice-Hall, 1960).

reread for answers. Read Danny his rights! Encourage him to ask good questions and show that you take him seriously every time he asks one. This is not so much like the old M&M routine. Here you show how you feel by answering appropriately on the level of the question. For example, the quickest way to put down questioning behavior is to respond to a serious question with a flip answer, and vice versa. If Danny asks, "How can I pass the spelling test Friday?", he doesn't want to hear, "You might tell the teacher you're writing in Portuguese."

Incidentally, there is a high correlation between what teachers think of their pupils and the number of questions the pupils ask. If Danny tunes out and sits like a stump, he will probably be written off as stupid, contrary, or both. If, on the other hand, he asks reasonably appropriate questions and maintains an attitude of attention, he will more than likely be thought of as a bright boy with a reading problem. Does Danny know this?

Danny can be programmed to ask questions—literally. At first you might need to help him formulate questions. Say, for example, that he's thinking of joining the Navy. After a rundown on his experiences with a Navy recruiter, ask Danny, "What do you still need to know before deciding to sign up?" Danny might say, "How much I'd get a month," or "What would happen if there's a war." Say, "OK, pretend I'm the recruiter. Ask me those questions." (It's particularly helpful to have a copy of the Navy pamphlet—or younger Danny's geography text—for this type of exercise.) It may also be necessary to hound him into actually asking the question. "Danny, I want you to ask that question tomorrow during your geography class. Force yourself to raise your hand and ask the question."

The rap session is particularly helpful here. Danny can compare notes on such important topics as (1) teachers or employers who really want you to ask questions, (2) a teacher or employer who would just as soon you asked questions after class or work, and (3) the number of questions asked and the results.

Building a New Image

It would be terribly naive to assume that young Danny wants to be categorized as a "student." Chances are very good that his reputation has been built on clowning, testing the limits, sports, or anything but being a student. On the other hand there may have been a few experiences in the classroom painful enough to convince him there might be a better way. One of these experiences may have been being called on for oral reading or being asked questions about materials he had supposedly read. There are all kinds of ways to avoid being put on the spot, some more ingenious than others.

For the younger Dannys of this world, stress "which guys don't get called on and why." Danny really may not understand that if he sat and looked at his book, turned work in on schedule, and maybe asked one question a day, he would probably be allowed to sit and listen. If Danny is consistently giving the appearance of inattention, the teacher will call on him more just to get him back on track. You can't change Danny into a student overnight, but you just might get him to try something different for a day or two—sort of an experiment in adult psychology.

Student Dannys usually have sure-fire systems for avoiding oral reading. One Danny I know well confided to me that he hasn't read aloud in two years. He always makes sure his book is open to the wrong page. Then, when called on, he says, "I don't have the place." Almost always the teacher will call on someone else. If, on the other hand, someone else is asked to show him the place, the other student will make a big thing about his not even being on the right page. At this point the teacher calls on someone else and leaves Danny strictly alone after that.

The adult Danny may respond to anything on the job involving reading or writing in much the same way. The printed page signals him to clown or to be inattentive, just as it did in the old school days. Unfortunately the boss may fail to see the humor in the proposed group health plan leaflet. The clerk at the union hall will probably be similarly unimpressed when Danny examines the chair rather than the application form.

Material like the above is good for rap sessions. A group member just might come up with something really constructive, something like this response to being called on to read: "I'd rather not. I learn better when I listen." The point is that Danny will be much more likely to follow a suggestion made by another Danny than one that comes from you.

Another painful situation may have been report card time, particularly for the athlete who must maintain eligibility. Sometimes Danny will attempt to act more like a student just to keep playing football or swim or whatever. *Note:* This is one of several good reasons for encouraging participation in sports. Two other major reasons are (1) if he achieves in sports the accomplishment can spill over so he feels a little more confident in the classroom as well, and (2) using up excess energy leaves him better equipped to sit and listen.

Turning in Neat Work

There are three main reasons for failing grades or D's. In the elementary grades they are (1) not acting like a student, (2) failing tests, and (3) not turning in work (in that order). In junior high they are (1) failing tests and not turning in work, and (2) not acting like a student (in that order). In senior high they are (1) not turning in work, (2) failing tests, and (3) not acting like a student.

This is not the place for an essay on relaxation of standards in the high schools. However, it's my observation that more students fail from not turning in work than from any other cause, including test scores. On the other hand, any pupil who turns in all assignments—regardless of their quality—is almost guaranteed a passing grade. Maybe this is because so few students turn in all their work these days that the teacher believes that Danny's effort means "Danny really cares about his grade." Generally this is followed by the thought, "I'll give him the benefit of the doubt, even though he did flunk the test."

It is to Danny's advantage to turn in every assignment and have it look good, even if the contents are short on quality. For example, if Danny's mother or father or brother or sister types his book report (usually this is legal, particularly if it is typed exactly like the rough draft), Danny will most probably get a B on it. This B will be given even though every third word is misspelled and Danny really only read the back cover, not the book. On the other hand, if Danny writes in pencil and turns in a smudged, crossed-out page torn out of a spiral binder, he will most probably get a D for the exact same report.

There are two morals to this parable. He will get a passing grade, even for the page that looks like he wrapped his sandwich in it, if he turns it in. On the other hand, fancy packaging can make a difference of two letter grades.

Fancy packaging is not all that hard to learn. If no one types and Danny hasn't learned to yet, he should write in pen, carefully—after he washes his hands—on a regular piece of notebook paper. If he really wants to dazzle them with footwork, he should write on plain onionskin paper ("see-through") over a piece of lined paper.

Danny should also copy as many charts, drawings, maps, and such as he can find. Better still he should jazz them up with colored marking pens. By all means he should put it all together in a folder and include a title page. All this can be done with Danny's unique written expression and spelling patterns, and he'll still come out way ahead of the game. (Just ask some of my university students. I've been a sucker for fancy packaging all my life and so are many other teachers.)

Although the above emphasizes Danny the student, there are implications for the adult Danny. For example, does he know that for a fee he can get any written work edited and typed? Does he know where to go for this? Presumably Danny is already enrolled in a typing class—but what if he needs a job résumé tomorrow? A lack of reading and writing skills can keep Danny in the same old rut while others move on to better jobs.

Do you object to working on appearances? You'll help Danny to read better and write better even without it. But while he's learning, why not encourage him to put his best foot forward?

Connected Reading

The situation in a nutshell is that Danny already has the word-attack skills he needs to read better. Simple practice in decoding at his decoding level is bound to increase his speed and accuracy. On the other hand, Danny's regular reading material is at frustration level. Unless you can present this reading in a nonthreatening manner, Danny will not increase speed and accuracy at this level. This is the story of his life so far—student Danny sits and worries about being called on to read out loud, so he doesn't even pick up information when someone else reads, and certainly doesn't try to use what he hears as a reading model. By the time he leaves school, nobody is reading out loud to him any more. Even if someone did, he wouldn't have a copy, so he can't follow along silently and improve his reading.

You may have a choice to make. You can have Danny read at decoding level, hoping he will increase speed and accuracy rapidly enough to take some of the heat off. Or you can help him read his assignments at frustration level, realizing that his reading skills may not increase as fast but that this approach may help keep him afloat in school or society. Ideally you will not have to make a choice. With luck, one person—tutor, parent, brother or sister, friend—will take the job of being Danny's talking book. This person will read all frustration-level assignments to him. A second person will work strictly at decoding level. In this manner Danny's reading skills will increase at optimal speed, and he can hang in there at school or in society while he's doing it.

If Danny can be conned into spending at least one half-hour per day reading, progress will, of course, be accelerated. The Dannys easiest to convince of the need for practice are the athletes, particularly swimmers and runners. They have seen what practice or the lack of it can do.

Often a short-term contract is the best method. Danny agrees to 30 minutes of reading a day for, say, two weeks, in addition to the tutoring sessions. At the end of that time, if you're both not happy with the amount of progress, it's back to the drawing board. At this point you might change any or all of the following: level of material, time spent per day, or use of a tape recorder for continued modeling. Make a new contract and try, try again.

Regardless of which type of connected reading you select for your sessions—decoding level or frustration level—Danny should receive an ironclad guarantee that he will not be asked to read orally by himself. (And just how often does the adult use oral reading?) Any testing of reading from here on out should be silent reading—hence, comprehension.

At Decoding Level

In the beginning of this book I told you quite a bit about finding decoding level with the 100-word method. This works if Danny is going to read orally by himself, but in Stage III he isn't. Now what? You will need materials on about third-grade level to start. Ask your librarian or a friendly teacher for some help. Put a selection down in front of Danny and have him read 100 words silently. When he comes to a word he can't figure out, have him tell you. That way you can still do a word count to find out if the book is on decoding level!

The Neurological Impress Method

This approach sounds impressive and does work very well with some problem readers. But despite its grand title, you don't need a college or high school education to use it.

Level with Danny right from the start that this isn't going to be a bowl of cherries, and he's really going to have to sweat a lot. But also explain:

- He isn't necessarily going to read the whole selection you've given him, unless it's very short.
- It's just for decoding practice to increase speed and ease.
- He will get out of this kind of book in short order, possibly in two weeks to a month.

What you do is provide Danny with material at decoding level. Set the book on the table. Seat Danny directly in front of the book, and seat yourself slightly behind him to one side. (You will need to reach the book without cutting off Danny's view of the material. Experiment a bit.) Explain to Danny that you are going to read the material out loud together. You will run your finger along the words, keeping the place, and he can listen to you if he doesn't know some of the words. However, he's to try his best to say what you say at the same time or with as short an interval in between as possible.

Since this is strictly decoding practice, you will not—I repeat, *not*—ask comprehension questions about the material. Assure Danny of this so he can concentrate strictly on listening to your words and repeating them as fast as he can. This is the best reading model, requiring the most participation from the pupil.

At first you will probably feel that you are dragging Danny through the pages. You may have to keep insisting that he speak louder and try harder. You may have to drop down to a lower reading level until he gains confidence. This method *is* worth your best shot, though. If it works, progress will be dramatic. Only 15 minutes a day for a month may result in advancing three grade levels. You must, however, be willing to keep pushing Danny upward in levels. Once he gets the hang of hard third-grade reading materials, which he could do in three days, you should move right into a harder book. At all times it is necessary to read with average to just slightly below average speed. If you read too slowly, you won't gain much.

If after two weeks of the 15-minute sessions you're still dragging him through the same level, then it's time to try variations. As I said, give it your best shot—but don't beat a dead horse either. Another reason for trying other methods is plain old variety. Even if the Neurological Impress Method works, you and Danny will need a breather now and then.

Variation 1.   In the most promising connected reading approach, Danny doesn't read with you but runs his finger along the lines as you are reading orally. This is probably what you should try if the Neurological Impress Method bombs out. Danny must read with you, if silently, to keep the place. He is physically involved, which is crucial for active people of all ages. You can easily check to see if he's with you by slowing down or speeding up.

Variation 2.   Here you read orally and keep the place with your own finger. Danny must agree to read silently at the same time. This is one of the most beneficial methods for reading at frustration level (described below), and isn't too bad for some people reading at their decoding level, either. Obviously it's harder to monitor whether Danny is really keeping up with you. The best way is to stop dead from time to time, pull your finger off, and ask Danny, "Where are we?"

Variation 3.   If Danny is older or if using your finger seems to insult him, try this. Read orally with neither of you keeping the place, and stop every so often to ask, "Where are we?" As long as he can tell you, things are going smoothly.

Variation 4.   Sometimes you might want to try reading incorrectly (a little of this goes a long way). If Danny picks up your errors, you're in business. You might want to alert him ahead of time that you will be making some mistakes—sort of a "catch me if you can" scene.

The Big Show

This is what you're leading up to with all the modeling activities: Danny is going to continue reading silently when the modeling stops. If you're a parent, sister or brother, or friend you might suddenly have to jump up and answer the phone or break up a cat fight. Hand Danny the book and tell him to keep going. If you're a teacher using the approach, you may suddenly have to attend to another student or some clerical detail, with the same result.

You may well be amazed at how easily all this comes about. Modeling is a means to an end, and that end is independence. The material you have been modeling has probably sunk in somewhat, even though comprehension was never mentioned. Often it's a blessed relief for Danny to be turned loose on something that he knows isn't too hard and that he's already familiar with, at least in part.

When you return after a short interval (from your cat fight or lesson plans), ask Danny how it's going. Then ask him whether or not he wants to continue reading silently, or if he would prefer more modeling. Most Dannys are pretty truthful about this. If he can handle it independently, he will probably elect to do so. If not, don't worry. He will get there. *Remember:* Don't feel you're not earning your keep if you just let Danny read silently. You are after independent reading, aren't you?

Frustration Level

There is a theory that works just often enough to drive educators bananas, whereby a Danny will be able to handle frustration-level reading on his own. Known as "hooked on books," it means that if Danny wants to read what's there badly enough, he'll drag himself through it—pulling himself up by his bootstraps in reading while he's at it.

The boy I told you about earlier—the one who hasn't read orally in two years—is currently attempting to digest an auto mechanics manual. This is a very individual thing and often requires an element of sneakiness or larceny to make it work. The system originated in a maximum security prison when the prisoners began stealing paperbacks from book carts. I read somewhere that a father of eight manages to trick most of his brood into reading classics, mainly by hiding them on a closet shelf.

You probably shoudn't try this approach in your sessions with Danny. The burning interest—and it must begin with him—must be strong enough to overcome the drudgery of decoding at frustration level. However, if you find out that Danny's reading something hard because he wants to, don't discourage him. If you hadn't heard of the hooked-on-books syndrome, your typical reaction to the boy with the auto mechanics manual might be, "Let me help you find a book on your decoding level." *Now* when he tells you he's reading the manual, you'll say "Oh, really?" and go on with something else. (Never make a big deal out of it. If you do and he has to give up on his hard reading, he'll feel guilty or dumb.)

Survival Reading

This is the other type of reading at frustration level that will have to be done by someone else—usually the parent, tutor, or teacher. It consists of the health assignment for Tuesday, the literature selection for English, the payroll savings plan information, and all the other day-to-day nitty-gritty Danny has to cope with in school or on the job. Survival reading was covered fairly completely in a previous section, "Help Outside the Reading Sessions." I mention it again here because it has top priority. If not done elsewhere, this material shoud be modeled during the connected reading session. You should stick to the less strenuous forms of modeling, however. Never do straight Neurological Impress on it. You are after comprehension, and Neurological Impress is strictly for ease and speed practice.

Beyond Connected Reading

The major purpose of the connected reading described in this section so far is to increase Danny's ease (accuracy) in reading. This smoothing out means he can read faster, make use of context, and pronounce the words more accurately. The more automatic this becomes to him, the better chance he has to comprehend what he decodes.

Obviously, however, some comprehension is involved even in modeling activities. Silent reading is the key. Once Danny can and does continue on his own when you go to answer the door, he's ready to begin a concentrated attack on comprehension. And now, patient tutor, we're finally ready for the greatest show of all: reading comprehension and how to help Danny do it.

Comprehension and Study Skills

Often Danny will be completely oblivious of the fact that able readers read in different ways to get different jobs done. This isn't so surprising, since Danny doesn't know the first thing about being an able reader. To him reading means plowing through material 1 word at a time. Danny will need to learn how to:

- read to find answers when questions are given
- read to find answers when questions aren't given
- deal with unfamiliar vocabulary
- translate what he has read into his own words
- remember what he has read in sequential order
- summarize what he has read
- combine things he has read in different sources
- reach a survival writing level

Reading to Find Answers

Danny's rate for regular connected reading will be steadily increasing; however, it will be a while before he can handle a tenth-grade to adult quesiton-and-answer assignment. Ideally the tutor will read all the material to Danny first (modeling), though this is not always possible. The chapter or pamphlet may be too long, leaving no time to answer questions, or the assignment or situation may require action before the next tutoring session. Danny must learn to get the job done himself. Very often survival in school or in the adult world is connected with finding answers to questions fast and reacting appropriately. Student Danny must write down the answers and turn them in; adult Danny must be able to repair the new-model machines.

When the Questions Are There

Turn to the questions under consideration and help Danny scan the first one, looking for key words. Give him just a second or two and then cover up the question. Ask him to tell you what he thinks the question is. After he has done this, have him read the question silently. Again, cover up the question; now ask him to tell you the question in his own words. If this is too hard for him, read the question to him and then have him read it silently.

Concentrating on the questions at the end of a textbook unit *before* reading the material will serve several purposes. The questions tend to use key words, so that Danny may study new vocabulary before touching the connected reading. Also most questions will provide an outline of sorts, giving an overview of the points to be covered. Finally it will help Danny get ready for the inevitable quiz by assuring him that he will be able to read the questions. (Most teachers are not particularly creative when it comes to test questions. Although they may not copy them word for word, there will be a great deal of similarity between text questions and test questions.)

Hunt the answer.   When Danny has demonstrated that he can repeat the first question in his own words, it's time to play "hunt the answer." Since authors, fortunately, tend to display a lack of creativity when it comes to the order of questions, there's every chance that the answer to the first question will be found on the first page or two of the chapter. Set Danny scanning—that's tracking line by line, or several lines at a time—looking for the key words. When he has found them, ask him again what the question is without looking back at it. If he is unable to do this, have him look at the question, keeping his finger in the place where he found the key words.

Next have Danny back up to the beginning of the paragraph or other prominent subdivision that contains the key words and read silently until he can answer the question. You will probably notice that Danny has a great deal of difficulty with this entire process, particularly remembering the question while he is searching for the answer. The second most common problem is not finding an answer appropriate for the question. Danny has probably been used to copying any sentence that has the key word or words in it.

This type of exercise makes a great group activity. If you want to jazz it up a bit you can have races for the various parts of the process. ("Which of you can tell me the question in your own words first? Ready . . . go." Or, "Let's see who can find the key words first. Begin.") Whatever else you do, be sure to spend quite a bit of time on reading to answer questions. Danny will need this skill again and again.

When the Questions Aren't There

Finding answers to questions that are given is a much easier task than reading to find answers when the questions aren't there. When Danny can answer given questions, he's ready to try "Here's the answer, now what's the question?"

The overview.   Take that leaflet on the new-model washers (make sure you know what it's about). Ask Danny to flip through it in about 60 seconds flat, concentrating on the table of contents, large-type subheadings, any illustrations, and about 5 words per page. Remove the leaflet and ask him, "What are some of the things this leaflet tells you about?" (This may take lots of encouragement to start. You probably will want to try a second scanning.)

Thinking of questions.   When Danny has a general idea of the content, concentrate on the first section or paragraphs. Have him scan the first section rapidly—in about 30 seconds. Then have him tell you the questions or important points he thinks this section covers. Write these down for Danny.

Reading for answers.   Now have him read the section silently at his regular rate. Working with Danny, check the questions or points you wrote down and revise them if necessary. Now ask the first question or state the first point and ask Danny to respond to it. Continue through the leaflet section by section.

This method is very helpful for several reasons. First, an overview of the entire contents puts the whole task in perspective. It's not so frightening when Danny has a general idea of the boundaries or limits. Then the notion of reading to answer questions—even his own—gives Danny a specific purpose for decoding.

Concentrating.   It's important to stress concentrating in a group situation. More often than not, Danny will need to answer questions in a noisy classroom or at the Department of Motor Vehicles while surrounded by loud conversationalists. Some Dannys will find it extremely helpful to cover their ears with their hands while scanning. (It's just the principle of the thing, since it really won't cut down on the noise so much.) Have Danny try using his index finger to mark his scanning progress since this will keep him physically involved with the task. For the same reason he might also whisper the key words as he scans.

Dealing with Unfamiliar Vocabulary

In Stage I a large part of each session was devoted to learning words. Many of these were basic utility words—words that the Stage I reader already used in speech. As Danny decodes on ever higher levels there will be more and more words that he doesn't use in speech, and many that he will not even recognize when he hears them.

It would be impractical to list all the unfamiliar words on cards and study them individually. Danny needs to know what to do when faced with an unfamiliar word when he's miles away from you and your cards. So you need to make some decisions about how important each unfamiliar word is. Listing or studying them all might well destroy Danny's confidence.

When deciding which vocabulary words to select for study, consider these points:

- Can Danny pronounce the words?
- Does the pronunciation help him with the meaning?
- Can Danny figure out what the word means without pronouncing it?
- Is the meaning the only thing that's really important here?
- Is the word important enough that pronunciation and meaning should both be stressed?

The answers to these questions will vary and can only be determined by the tutor on the spot. For example, suppose that Danny is going to read a TV magazine write-up of a Lou Gehrig movie. While Danny is reading silently you will notice several words or terms that are probably unfamiliar to him: *incurable, amyotrophic lateral sclerosis, formidable obstacle.* Which ones would Danny recognize if he could pronounce them? Probably *incurable* and *obstacle.* After Danny reads the selection, point to *incurable* and ask him to say the word. If he can't pronounce it, remind him of the word-attack skills he should use (Stage II, page 65). When he can pronounce the word, ask him what it means. If he doesn't know and you think *incurable* is important, talk about it.

You probably decided that Danny will never see *amyotrophic lateral sclerosis* again (it is a rare condition!). So see if Danny can get some meaning from the term without pronouncing it. The sentence reads, "Gehrig finds out that he has amyotrophic lateral sclerosis." Read the sentence up to the 3-word term and stop. Point to the three words and ask, "What do you suppose this is?" You're looking for an answer like "a sickness" or "a disease." Encourage anything that even comes close. Then leave it with "I can't pronounce it either" (if true).

As for *formidable,* you will make an arbitary decision whether to work on pronunciation, meaning, or both, or neither. This decision will be based on your estimate of how important this word is to Danny. Is he going to run into it often? Is it worth the time and effort? Unless the word appears fairly consistently in his reading, or at the very least in his listening vocabulary, it will self-destruct in short order. People don't have much luck storing words to use some time in the far distant future.

Translating What He Has Read

Retelling, sequencing, and summarizing are skills that I have already mentioned. Danny needs more than the mere mention of them, however. When the time comes for a book report or a similar activity, you'll see what I mean.

Retelling. Successful translation requires keeping in mind an overview of the content, reducing it down to the bone, and being able to retell it in your own words. Danny may be in trouble on the very first of these necessities. If the material is on frustration level, 80 percent or more of his effort is required just to decode the separate words, so he can't hold onto the general meaning. If the material must be on frustraton level—the book was assigned by the English teacher or the Internal Revenue Service sent it—do the modeling scene. Read it to him. For best results, tell him ahead of time that you will expect him to be able to retell the story or instructions in as few words as possible. (Stress this throughout all the translation activities.)

Sequencing. If Danny has trouble sequencing events, go back to the oral retelling of TV programs, work up to radio programs, and finally to modeled reading and silent reading. The shorter the material, the easier it should be to sequence. Sometimes Dannys who have spent most of their lives answering recall questions ("What time did Bill leave to go to the store?") need to be carefully led into sequencing. Do it for him a time or two if necessary. By all means select short stories on decoding level if you have a choice. As we have seen, the world outside doesn't always give you a choice.

Summarizing. If you think Danny had trouble sequencing or holding on to an overview, wait till you get to summarizing or cutting it to the bone. Danny usually believes that every golden word will be important. How else could they have given him so much trouble all these years? When you work with shorter units like a paragraph or a few sentences, make a big thing out of saying them over again in as few words as possible. This is another good activity for group work ("Who can say it in the fewest words?")

"Name That Paragraph" is an old favorite on reading achievement tests and may be one way to go. The tests contain short units especially suited to summarization. Danny may be amazed to learn how many extra words the typical selection contains. For the time being, retelling in short narrative style is more useful than "Name That Paragraph." Naming is more important for outlining and note taking, described later.

Encouragement.   If you're stressing retelling in his own words for the activities above, asking Danny to give you a short playback of the entire story should not present too many problems. (It shouldn't, but it sometimes does.) Sequencing problems are most often related to anxiety, and who is more anxious than Danny? Give him plenty of time and lots of encouragement as he progresses. There's another gambit in behavior modification that is useful here. It's called by many names, sometimes *successive approximation*. What it means is that if Danny even comes close to what you expect of him, you let it go with encouragement. (Encouragement can just be stopping the exercise with an "OK.") Maybe you need to examine your expectations if Danny constantly falls short. People who pride themselves on their translation abilities are probably the last people who should work with Danny.

Before leaving translation activities it is very important that you give Danny a model for translation. If you are reading frustration-level material to him, stop every so often and say, "What that means is. . . ." Give it to him in the kind of language he speaks.

Summarizing and Outlining

Note taking.   Depending upon how painful it is for Danny to write, this exercise may never leave the mental note-taking level. Start by giving Danny a short lecture, telling him ahead of time that you will ask him the following questions:

"What was I talking about in 1 to 5 words?" (summarization)

"In short form, what did I say?" (sequencing-translation)

"What test questions would I ask about it?" (judgment)

"What are the most important points I made?" (judgment)

This is the first exercise that has much to do with developing pupil judgment. Obviously it is superimportant for Danny to be able to sort the chaff from the wheat since he may get bogged down trying to retain every little thing. Unless he has a photographic memory (fat chance!), he will need to make automatic choices about what to save.

Writing notes will probably only get in the way of the selection process at first. If he starts worrying about how to get something down fast enough, he will miss the next point or two completely. A tape recorder might be helpful. Record what happens when Danny listens to your questions and then responds. Play it back and he can monitor his efforts.

Note taking (underlining) in a book.   Librarians, look the other way, please. If you have to use books on loan—like pupil texts—use a soft #2 pencil and an art gum or pink rubber eraser. (The one on the end of the pencil will not do the trick!) Have Danny go through the material underlining the important stuff (his choice). Be specific: Under no circumstances is he to underline more than 2 words per sentence. These must be important words that remind him of what the sentence says. Ideally he won't have to underline more than 4 to 6 words per paragraph. When you get to a certain point, like the end of a section, have Danny retell the material by looking at the words he underlined.

This activity is so important that every parent or teacher should try to supply Danny with books that don't have to be returned. (Either that or you can just pay for them at the end of the year.) College students have been doing this type of condensing and note taking since time immemorial, and who needs it more, the college student or Danny? Of course if you can't afford the books, your alternative is to insist that Danny erase his markings after taking the test on a chapter. If he has his own books, however, the sky's the limit on this activity. Marking pens and highlighters (pens that produce transparent color right over the print) will do a lot for Danny's morale.

Some people respond well to numbering important points in the margins. If the book already has center heads and side heads, a few numbers to indicate underlined material will give you a fairly respectable outline. Just how far Danny will want to go with this is anybody's guess. However, just numbering the phrases he underlines will probably help him remember the material.

Writing

What we have been mainly concerned with to date is the comprehension of material—the type of activity Danny would need to study for a test on Monday or to get ready to write that report. Unfortunately there is many a slip betwixt the reading and the writing. Even though this book is concerned with reading, it's not fair to leave Danny without some writing abilities. Even adult Danny will need to write work orders and notes to himself and others.

It's probably realistic to combine this session with the comprehension we've been talking about. That is, don't set your timer for 10 minutes and move arbitrarily to written expression when it rings. Writing and comprehension can be complementary in many respects, particularly when Danny has a reading assignment due on Thursday or an application to fill out by tomorrow.

Writing Answers to Questions

As usual, start on the oral level—that is, have Danny frame the answers to questions, using the process described earlier. But then pull a fast one. Write Danny's answer in his own words. (Language experience fanatics, take note!) Let him look at it for a short period of time. Then take back the answer and have Danny write it from dictation. If it bothers you that Danny does not express himself in complete sentences, work on this orally before you begin the writing from dictation.

Writing from dictation provides the same kind of valuable experience that modeling for reading does. Danny's decoding level for writing is bound to be way down there. He needs to study correct spelling and formation on this level rather than continue to produce errors indefinitely. *Note:* Don't forget the typing! This will probably work even better.

The Ultimate Hassle: The Research Report

When you were in school you probably learned that to prepare a research report you should first find a number of references; scan them to select appropriate sections; read and take notes on index cards; arrange the index cards in order; write an outline, rough draft, and don't forget the bibliography. But Danny has one duece of a time getting any information from one source, let alone several. Organization of material on this level will be completely beyond him for some time. So what do you do? After all, this report is worth a third of his grade. (Adult Danny can thank his stars that he probably won't have to worry about this kind of problem.)

Here's What You Do

Find two or three sources that aren't too far over Danny's head. Very simple encyclopedia articles are ideal for this. (The fewer and thinner the volumes, the simpler the encyclopedia!) Do the reading and make a mental outline of appropriate subsections. On index cards, write questions that when answered in sentence form will make up the report. Also write the page numbers where the answers to the questions can be found. Better yet, do this and stick the cards in the right pages. Number the cards. The answer to the question on card number 1 will be the first sentence of Danny's report, followed by the answer to question number 2, then 3, and so on.

   In this manner Danny will be able to handle the body of the report in the same way he attacks study questions. Stress formulating answers in sentences and in his own words. If he needs to run an answer by you orally before he writes it down, let him do so.

   When Danny can follow this procedure fairly easily (in about two reports), he's ready to try the next stage. Supply the material as before, preread it, and get a general idea of what's coming up. Indicate in the sources the material that seems most appropriate. Do this with very light pencil marks. Mark the pages with index cards. This time, don't write questions on the index cards, only the sequence number. (Number 1 means "Do this first," and so on.)

When Danny can find important information and get it down in the proper sequence, he's already up with the crowd in terms of writing reports and maybe way ahead if he has learned to write in his own words. At this point he's ready to try doing his own selecting and sequencing. Give Danny all the help he needs in sequencing. For example, he may well want to discuss with you, "Should symptoms come before treatment?" or "Maybe I should talk about what Russia's like now, then go back to the Czar."

A word of encouragement for you as helper is definitely in order here. Danny will probably only have to write three or four research reports in his entire school career. My youngsters suffered through a short epidemic of them starting in fifth or sixth grade and ending at about ninth grade. One a year was usually all the teacher could handle, with the exception of one masochist who assigned three in one year.

Danny On His Own

Gradually Danny will take the responsibility for his own reading progress. More of his reading will be done silently and his reactions to what he's read will be largely self-monitored. Both of you will realize that there are others waiting in the wings—other Dannys or Alices or Joes who need your time more. As Danny exits stage right, you'll both be eager to keep moving forward.

A Final Word

A book doesn't just stop as a rule, but then this book doesn't fit many rules that I know of. You'll be disappointed to learn that I didn't get that essay test made up to hear about your reading experience. Tell you what. You just go to work on Joe, Alice, and Danny and we'll call it a day. Good luck!

ABOUT THE AUTHOR

Dr. Judith H. Dettre works with problem readers in the Learning Laboratory at the University of Nevada, Las Vegas campus. She is on the faculty of the College of Education's Special Education Department and teaches graduate and undergraduate courses in learning disabilities. Her involvement with learners with special needs and their parents and friends spans a quarter of a century. Dr. Dettre has taught first, second, fourth, sixth, and eighth graders in regular classes; has taught learning-disabled, emotionally disturbed, and physically handicapped youngsters in special classes; and has tutored scores of problem readers of all ages. In her work she has given parents, friends, and teachers of problem readers the knowledge they need to carry on an effective reading-tutoring program alone. That knowledge and advice became this book.

Read For Meaning

PACEMAKER BESTELLERS®

"BesTellers are fantastic . . . the best source of free-reading materials
for my junior high remedial students. My concern is that they are
reading them all so feverishly that soon they will be looking for more."

Junior High School Teacher

Flight to Fear! Escape from Tomorrow! Night of Fire and Blood! The
appeal of these 30 award-winning books is obvious and immediate: they
are designed and written in the style of the best-selling paperbacks familiar to your students, complete with four-color covers and alluring excerpts
on the back. Together with the books' vivid illustrations, these features
invite your students to explore the popular themes of science fiction, mystery, suspense, adventure, and romance. The main characters are attrac-
tive young adults with whom they will readily identify.

Three sets of **BesTellers**® are now available at the same easy reading
level, grade 3.0. The Teacher's Guide offers plot summaries, helpful
teaching suggestions, vocabulary data, and comprehensive questions. The
BesTellers® Reading Program consists of two parts. Part I includes 30
Activity Cards (one per title) providing comprehension and interpretation
questions for students reading at third- and fourth-grade levels and a
Teacher's Guide. Part II—the BesTellers® Reading Checks—is a book of
60 duplicatable MAKEMASTER® worksheets (two per title) containing
simple objective exercises. BesTellers® I, II, and III: Complete Sets (four
copies each of 30 titles in rotating display units, plus Teacher's Guides);
5371-1. BesTellers® Reading Program: 5286-3. Each set of BesTellers®
and each part of the BesTellers® Reading Program is also available
separately.

Read For Growth

LAURA BREWSTER BOOKS™ Lisa Eisenberg

Whodunit! When it comes to insurance fraud, Laura Brewster is one investigator who gets the job done—no matter what. She also keeps your reluctant readers turning the pages, from one do-or-die cliffhanger to the next. With her trusty dog Nightshade and her green parrot Ringo, Laura travels all over the world—Mexico, Hollywood, London, Hong Kong—getting to the bottom of an amusement park murder here, the mysterious death of a rock star there. Though the odds are always against her, Laura's quick thinking and martial arts skills never fail to get her through. She's her own woman, successfully doing an almost impossible job. Complete Series (six titles plus Teacher's Guide): 1080-X

SPACE POLICE™ Leo P. Kelley

Fantastic, action-packed tales of space-age cops and robbers! Students who have never willingly cracked a book will quickly lose themselves in these imaginative plots, traveling through different dimensions of time and space—and meaning. The books' provocative themes—crime does not pay, jealousy in marriage, the generation gap, prejudice—provide an excellent basis for classroom discussion, and help your students to understand the variety of human values and motives. Even your poorest readers will read these six books with ease, because a third-grade reading level is all it takes to zoom off with the Space Police. Complete Series (six titles plus Teacher's Guide): 6376-8

JIM HUNTER BOOKS Ben Butterworth and Bill Stockdale

Are your nonreaders hungry for action? Give them British secret agent Jim Hunter—the new James Bond! From the steamy jungles of South America to the snowy mountains of Canada to the scorching deserts of the Middle East, Jim uses midget submarines, miniaturized electronic transmitters, and jet backpacks to thwart the arch-villain Bratt and his evil schemes. Lavish illustrations reinforce each book's story line, and the reading level gradually increases through the series (grade 1.0-3.0). Boxed Set (12 titles plus Teacher's Guide): 3780-5

By All Means, READ!

GALAXY 5™ SPACE PACK Leo P. Kelley

This six-book series of space fantasy adventures is sure to spark the interest of your unmotivated readers. The books feature fascinating characters —murderous robots, beautiful space pirates, evil kings—and exciting plots and events—space fever, mysterious forces, and underground cities. Imaginative cover and text illustrations vividly picture outer space. A special feature of the Space Pack is the set of DramaTape™ cassettes. Using a "radio show" format—complete with a cast of actors, background music, and sound effects—DramaTapes bring to life the first two chapters of each book. Space Pack (six titles, three DramaTapes, and Teacher's Guide): 3208-0

LIFELINE™ Tana Reiff

Here's an innovative way to introduce your students to decision making and problem solving. **LifeLine** books combine a controlled reading level (grade 1.0-3.0) with high-interest fiction about the real concerns of adults. In each of the seven books, the characters must face a particular problem and make decisions toward solving that problem. A unique feature of **LifeLine** is the "natural word groupings" of the text. Current studies in linguistics and psycholinguistics show that natural word breaks between lines, rather than random breaks required to justify columns, make a passage easier to read. The comprehensive LifeLine Curriculum Guide: Reading, Writing, and Life Skills, contains plot summaries, vocabulary data, comprehension questions, and 35 language-related activities on duplicatable MAKEMASTER® worksheets, each accompanied by teaching strategies and exercise objectives. Class Set (10 copies each of seven titles, plus one Curriculum Guide): 4324-4